RITES
OF PASSAGE

Jacqueline Dineen

Illustrated by Robert Ingpen
Consultant: Philip Wilkinson

Chelsea House Publishers
Philadelphia

First published in the United States in 1999

Dragon's World Ltd
Limpsfield
Surrey RH8 0DY
Great Britain

First published by Dragon's World Ltd, 1995

Text and captions by **Jacqueline Dineen**
based on *A Celebration of Customs & Rituals of the World*
by Robert Ingpen and Philip Wilkinson.

Editor: Diana Briscoe
Designer: Megra Mitchell
Art Director: John Strange
Design Assistants: Victoria Furbisher
and Karen Ferguson
Editorial Director: Pippa Rubinstein

ISBN 0 7910 5133 1

Typeset in Bembo, Garamond and
Opti-Announcement by Dragon's World Ltd
Printed in Italy

Contents

Introduction

None of us knows exactly what the future holds for us. We make choices about some things, but other things are outside our control. Life is an adventure of discovery, because it is impossible to look ahead and plan everything. But there are some things we can be certain about. To come into the world, we have to be born. At the end of our lives, we will die. In between, with luck, we will grow through childhood to become adults, and begin to take responsibility for our own lives. Maybe we will marry and have children of our own. And so the cycle of life continues....

For thousands of years, people the world over have marvelled at these happenings. The birth of a baby seems like a miracle. That baby is a complete individual who is different from anyone else on Earth. Even though there are millions of people in the world, no two are exactly alike. From earliest times, people have feared death. What is it like? What happens afterwards? It is the one thing which we cannot explain because no one can tell us about it. For centuries people have wondered who makes these things happen and who controls our lives.

In their search for answers to these questions, people developed many different beliefs. Most of these were based on religion. Ancient peoples worshipped many gods who they believed controlled their destinies from the moment they were born until the day they died, and beyond. Most ancient civilizations believed that they would have an afterlife, and that their reception when they arrived in this new life depended on the way they had behaved on Earth.

Today, people all over the world still observe many rituals for these major happenings in their lives. The birth of a new baby is celebrated with joy. The rituals for protecting a young baby are very different, but their aims are the same – to ward off evil spirits and give the parents peace of mind. When these have been carried out, the parents feel that they have done all they can to ensure the child's good health and fortune.

When a child reaches adulthood, parents may introduce him or her into society with a coming-of-age or initiation ceremony. In many communities, one of the biggest celebrations is at the time when a child becomes an adult. It may be a practical moment when parents acknowledge that the young person is able to take responsibility for their actions. In some societies, the young person has to go through an ordeal or feat of bravery. The age at which a person becomes an adult also varies. In some societies, people

are regarded as adults as young as twelve or thirteen. In other places, they have to wait until they are twenty or thirty years old.

The customs associated with marriage are often colourful and may be strange. In some cultures, people worry that the Evil Eye will ruin everything at a wedding, just as it might at the birth of a baby. So this is another time for elaborate precautions to fool the spirits into thinking that nothing out of the ordinary is going on.

The rituals surrounding death prepare the dying person for what may happen to them, and help the people left behind to come to terms with the loss of a loved one. The time between death and the funeral varies in different societies and religions. Jewish law states that people should be buried within twenty-four hours of death if possible. In other societies, the body is not buried or cremated until it has lain in the family house for some time. Many cultures believe that it is necessary to guard a body at all times until the funeral. This is known as 'keeping vigil'. A vigil also helps people to get used to the fact that the person is dead. The thought of a dead body can seem frightening, but if people can see it and get used to it lying there, it may help them to accept the death.

All these rituals, known as 'rites of passage', are steeped in ancient tradition. But why do we practise them? In this book, we travel around the world looking at the different ways in which these celebrations are carried out and their particular relevance to the people concerned. What we shall find is that, although we are all different, we are all very much the same in our beliefs about these crucial matters and the way in which we react to them.

Birth

Every animal has to bear young for life to continue. Yet the birth of a baby is still one of the most miraculous happenings. As a mother gazes on her new-born infant, she knows that here is a unique new individual. However many babies are born in the world on the same day, no one else will be just like her baby.

Most parents also feel a great sense of responsibility mingled with the joy. They know that ahead of them lie many years of bringing up the child as best they can. How will they cope with the new infant? What sort of a life can he or she look forward to? Will they be able to provide for the child and bring it up to be a happy and fulfilled adult?

Parents and family are aware that they are responsible for the shaping of this new life. The anxiety of waiting is mixed with excitement for both parents. They begin to plan for the baby's arrival and buy new things for the nursery.

MOST SOCIETIES HAVE *their own customs for welcoming a new baby to the world. The baby will be too young to know what is going on, of course, but once the rituals have been completed, the parents know that he or she is now a recognized member of society.*

Welcome to the World

Most societies have their own customs for welcoming a new baby to the world. The welcoming ritual for a new baby may be very simple – perhaps just cards and messages of congratulations from friends and family.

Flowers are often sent to a new mother and people may send gifts of clothes and toys. All these actions show that people are thinking of the new baby.

Some people hold religious ceremonies which include giving the baby a name. There may be a party where people celebrate with food, drink and music. But whatever form it takes, welcoming a baby into the world is always a joyous occasion.

As the days pass, the expectant mother wonders whether everything will be all right. Will the baby be healthy? Will the birth go well?

Boy or Girl?

People have devised many weird and wonderful ways of trying to predict whether a baby is a boy or a girl. One of the strangest must be the old Welsh custom of hanging the charred bone from a shoulder of mutton in the doorway of the house. Once the bone was in place, the baby would be the same sex as the next person who walked through the door. As there was a fifty-fifty chance of being right, this method probably worked some of the time!

Another way was by hanging the mother's wedding ring by a thread over her stomach. If the ring swung in circles, the baby would be a girl; if it went from side to side, you could expect a boy.

Preparing for the Birth

One reason that a birth is such a cause for celebration is that it follows months of anxiety, particularly for the mother. In western societies, much of the mystique has been been taken out of childbirth. Everything is carefully planned and the mother's progress is monitored every step of the way. She visits her local hospital for check-ups to see how the baby is developing. She is bombarded with advice on what she should eat, how

pregnancy are advised to stop some of their activities, to take it easy and 'put their feet up' until the birth. But in some cultures, the women are expected to go on working right up to the time they give birth.

The !Kung people are hunters and gatherers who live in the Kalahari Desert in Africa. Women are the main food collectors of the tribe. Each woman, even if she is pregnant, will go out with the other women and bring home just as much food, even though she may be lumbering under the weight of a baby that is just about to be born.

THE !KUNG WOMEN *continue to gather food almost until the moment of birth. The men are too busy hunting to take on this extra duty.*

much exercise she should take, and what she should and should not do during her pregnancy. But even with all the benefits of modern medicine and knowledge, things can still go wrong. She will try to imagine what life will be like when there is another person in the house. What will the new arrival be like? Will it be a boy or a girl? As the months go by, the mother can feel the baby moving inside her. She knows that it is already a living human being and soon it will be born.

Many of the preparations for the birth are concerned with the mother's health. As she gets bigger it is more difficult for her to get around and she begins to feel very tired. In many societies, mothers nearing the end of

Fit or Fat?

It is often said that an expectant mother has to eat for two, but this may just make her fat if she is not careful what she eats. The idea of a properly balanced diet may seem a modern one but in fact people have long realized the importance of eating the right foods and have traditions about them.

In western societies, this usually means eating enough of each type of food to make sure that no nutrients or vitamins are lacking. In other cultures, it is important to eat equal amounts of opposite types of foods to achieve a balanced diet.

A Chinese doctor would advise a balance between yin (negative) and yang (positive) foods. In parts of India, a woman would be told to eat equal amounts of 'hot' and 'cold' foods. She might also be advised to turn down gifts of rich foods in case her body could not tolerate them.

In Central America, the terms 'hot' and 'cold' do not necessarily refer to the temperature or spiciness of the food. In Guatemala, for example, a pregnant woman is thought to be in a very 'hot' state and so should avoid 'hot' foods such as honey, the herb oregano and certain vegetables. On the other hand, she should not eat very 'cold' foods, such as beans or pork, as the contrast might make her catch cold.

Many pregnant women have a craving for certain foods, even things which they do not usually like. Guatemalan women are told to eat anything they crave for as this is the baby's way of asking for some particular food.

IN CENTRAL AMERICA, *pregnant women avoid foods that are very 'hot' or very 'cold'.*

Learning to be a Mother

The expectant mother knows that once her baby is born, she will have her work cut out coping with its demands. There will be no time to look up a book every time the baby cries or needs its nappy changed.

So another part of the preparation period is learning how to look after a young baby. In western societies, pregnant women go to special classes to learn about childbirth and what to do when the baby has been born.

In traditional societies, mothers do not have formal classes and it is left to the older women of the family or village to tell them what they need to know. Sometimes a midwife (someone who is trained to help with the birth of babies) will be there to instruct and help new mothers.

Fathers

A few years ago in most societies, fathers did not expect to take much of an active role in looking after a young baby beyond pushing the pram occasionally.

Today, things have changed in many western societies and fathers tend to become more involved with day-to-day child care. So it is quite common to see fathers at the preparation classes as well as mothers. They learn breathing exercises and other techniques to help their wives during labour.

· Childbirth in New Guinea ·

The Hua people who lived in the highlands of Papua New Guinea believe that women are polluted or impure during the whole of the time that they are young enough to bear children because of the blood associated with childbirth. When a woman has a child and some of the blood flows out of her body, she becomes a bit less polluted until, by the time she reaches old age, she may have lost all her pollution and become completely pure. A newly married woman is thought to be very polluted and no men or older women are allowed to eat any food she has prepared in case the pollution spreads to them.

DIET

Hua women who are pregnant are advised to eat certain foods and avoid others. A strict diet is thought to help against pollution. Greasy or slippery foods such as pig fat, frogs and some types of vegetables and mushrooms are supposed to help the baby slip out of the mother's body more easily. But any foods that may make the mother's womb dry out, such as some types of yam and bananas, are to be avoided at all costs. The mother should not eat burned tubers (the swollen roots of some vegetables) as these might make the baby stick in the womb in the same way that burnt food sticks to the cooking pot.

EASING THE BIRTH

The woman takes other steps to help 'slipperiness' and so help the delivery of the baby. She sits in water which is supposed to wash up into her body and make the baby slippery. A spell is recited over the mother to help.

THE NURSING MOTHER

When a baby has been born, the mother is advised to eat foods which help her flow of milk for feeding the baby. Foods which help the flow of milk include pig fat, sugar cane and cucumber. If the mother's milk is already flowing well, she need not worry too much about eating them.

• Childbirth among the Masai •

The Masai are a nomadic people who live in East Africa. They depend on their herds of sheep and cattle for food and the importance of these animals is reflected in many of their rituals. Early in her pregnancy, a Masai woman eats a normal diet, but she gradually changes some of the foods as time goes by. She may avoid milk in case it makes the baby fat and the delivery more difficult. She is also careful not to eat diseased or undercooked meat to avoid bacteria and parasites. These precautions are sound common sense.

make a mock attempt to draw blood from a bullock. If the baby is a boy, the instructions to the father are reversed.

THE BIRTH
The baby is born at home. The mother is usually helped by an older woman from her family who acts as midwife. When the baby has been delivered, the midwife cuts the umbilical cord, saying 'You are responsible for your life, as I am responsible for mine'. Child and mother are washed in water and milk.

BOY OR GIRL?
The father has to keep away while the mother is giving birth. When the baby has arrived, the midwife calls to him. If the baby is a girl, she tells him to draw blood from the jugular vein (the main vein in the neck) of a heifer or young cow. The father must also

FEASTS AND BLESSINGS
The father brings the blood he has drawn which is mixed with milk to make a drink for the mother. Then a ram is slaughtered inside the mother's house and eaten by the women. After the feast, the women sing prayers of blessing. Next day, a sheep is killed and the midwife is given the best cut of meat. Its fat is melted down to make a drink for the mother. Usually, the child is named soon after birth. The mother dresses in her best skirt of lambskin decorated with beads, and all her earrings and necklaces. The elders and women decide on a name and bless the baby saying, 'May that name dwell in you.'

The Baby is Born

Until recently, children were always born in great privacy in all cultures. The mother was helped by a midwife or a doctor but no one else was allowed into the room during the birth. In some societies, the mother could only be seen by other women so even a male doctor was not allowed. In western societies today, the father is often present during the birth. This makes him feel that he is taking a greater part in the birth of his child instead of hovering anxiously outside the door, and he can help and support the mother. But in other cultures, privacy and seclusion for the mother is still observed.

Earlier this century, there were reports of women in West Africa disappearing into the bush and having the baby without any help. However, it is more common for mothers to be helped by other women.

PROTECTING A CHILD FROM THE SPIRIT WORLD

The rituals for protecting a young baby are very different, but their aims are the same – to ward off evil spirits and give the parents peace of mind. When these rituals have been carried out, the parents can feel that they have done all in their power to ensure the child's good health and fortune.

ROMANIA

In the Balkans (south-eastern Europe), there are several traditional rituals for warding off the 'Evil Eye'. In Romania, it was the custom to bathe a new baby in hot water and mark its forehead with a small spot of white ashes. After the bath, the water was poured away very carefully to avoid spilling any on the spirits.

SPAIN

In northern Spain, new-born babies are laid on a mattress and a man leaps over them. His leap in the air is a symbol of the dangers the children face in life and his safe landing on the ground is a sign that they will escape from danger.

Warding off Evil Spirits

For centuries, people have been afraid of evil spirits and many ancient customs were concerned with protecting mother and baby from them. In European countries, before the days of modern hospital care, babies were delivered by a midwife who was a far cry from the highly trained midwife of today.

She was probably simply a local woman who had mastered a few herbal remedies and knew a bit about babies. When she was called to a woman who was about to give birth, her first task was go round the house, untying any knots she could find. This was to help the mother to relax so that the birth would be easier. Then she locked and bolted all doors and windows to keep the evil spirits out.

In India, a knife was put under the mother's bed as added protection against the spirits. In Greece, it was believed that women who were having a child would fall prey to the 'Evil Eye' unless strict precautions were taken. All mirrors were removed from the room so that the mother could not cast the 'Evil Eye' on herself by looking into one.

JAPAN
Japanese fathers sometimes perform a kite-flying ritual after the birth of a child. If the kite soars into the air without any trouble, the child will have a similarly trouble-free life.

AUSTRALIA
The custom of 'baby-smoking' practised by Aboriginals is designed to protect the child by giving it strength from the land, symbolized by the leaves and wood of the konkerberry tree.

IRELAND
An Irish father would stay with the new baby for several days and nights to protect it from evil spirits.

Once the baby had been born, the mother had to stay in at night until it was baptised, as she was still at risk from the spirits.

Women often died during childbirth, usually because there were no medicines. But if a woman or her baby did die, this was the fault of evil spirits. In northern India, people believed that a woman who died within ten days of having a baby became an evil spirit herself. In the north of England, people used to think it was unlucky to tread on the grave of an unbaptized child.

Dangers All Around

In many traditional societies, people still have a healthy respect for the spirits and the havoc they can wreak, even in cultures where childbirth has the reputation of being trouble-free. In fact, the image of a woman disappearing into the countryside and returning with a baby is probably greatly exaggerated. Among traditional societies there is still a belief that things can go wrong and if they do, the spirits are to blame.

The Lele people of Zaire believe that both mother and unborn child are in danger from the forest spirits. They also believe that the unborn child is a threat to others while it is still in the womb. A pregnant Lele woman avoids contact with anyone who is sick in case the unborn child makes the illness worse.

The Makuna people of the southwestern Amazon also believe that dangerous spirits are waiting to harm them. Before a birth, the father asks the local shaman (medicine man) to carry out special magic rituals to protect the parents and the child from the spirits.

Back into Circulation

After the birth, the mother needs a few days to rest and recover, particularly if it is her first baby. In western societies, she may stay in hospital for a short while, learning more about how to look after her new baby.

In India, followers of the Hindu religion belong to different castes or social classes. A woman is thought to be impure for different lengths of time, depending on her caste. Members of the highest caste, the priestly

REMOVING INAUSPICIOUSNESS

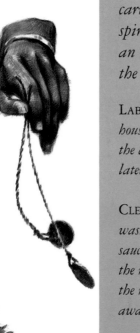

In northern India, a complicated series of rituals is carried out to protect mother and child from evil ancestor spirits who might do them harm. Each ritual transfers an ill omen away from the mother, so that the baby has the best start in life.

LABOUR: *While the mother is in labour, the women from the household circle one-rupee coins over her. This is supposed to speed up the delivery and protect the mother from the spirits. The coins are later given to the wife of the Brahman (priest).*

CLEANSING: *When the baby has been born, a female relative washes the mother's breasts to purify them. She then brings a small saucer of milk containing some blades of grass. She puts a coin into the mixture and then uses the blades of grass to sprinkle milk on to the mother's breasts. When she has finished, she takes the coin away, which removes the influence of dangerous ancestor gods.*

OFFERINGS: *On the sixth day after the birth, the midwife performs a ceremony to the goddess Bemata, who is believed to have placed the baby in the mother's womb. Grain is placed on a tray and covered with a cloth. Sugar and flour are put on to another tray. A lamp filled with mustard oil is placed at the head end of the cot and five heaps of fried bread are laid out, one for each leg of the cot and one for the goddess. A rough image of Bemata is made out of cow dung and wrapped in a cloth. The mother squats by the cot with the child in her arms and some grain is handed to her. Then she makes an offering to the goddess.*

Naming the Baby

The most important ritual for welcoming the new baby into the world is a naming ceremony. This may be religious, although it need not be.

In the Christian religion, babies are baptised and named in church during the first few months of life.

It used to be customary to immerse the child totally in the font of holy water as a reminder of Christ's baptism in the River Jordan. However, this procedure often led to howls of protest from the infant in question and it has been abandoned in many churches. It is now more usual for the priest to dip his hand into the font of holy water and make the sign of the cross on the child's forehead, naming him or her at the same time.

Christian parents normally ask two or

IN EUROPE, A *new mother used to go through a religious ceremony known as 'churching'.*

Brahmans, are impure for ten days, but for women of lowlier castes it is forty days. But all women are confined for a period of forty days, whichever caste they belong to.

The custom of 'mother roasting' is practised in the Philippines. A fire is built on hot rocks and the mother lies near it for a week. Water is poured on the fire to make steam which purifies her.

On Palau, an island in the Pacific Ocean, the mother lives apart from everyone else for four days after she has had her baby. During this time, the midwife bathes her eight times each day with a mixture of coconut oil and a spice called turmeric. After this ritual bathing, she is thought to be pure enough to return to general society.

Baptism

A baby often bawls its head off during a baptism ceremony, much to the embarrassment of its parents. But at one time in England, this would have been seen as a good sign because it was thought to be bad luck if a baby did not cry during the ceremony.

three close friends or relations to be godparents to the baby. The godparents take part in the baptism service, at which they promise to look after the child if anything happens to the parents and to bring the child up in the Christian way.

A new form of naming ceremony has recently been introduced for parents who do not practise religion, but still want to mark the arrival of a baby in some way. Friends and relations gather for the ceremony which can be held at the parents' home or in a larger place such as an hotel or a hall. Instead of

godparents, the baby has patrons who make similar promises to look after the child should anything happen to the parents.

Other cultures also use one of the elements in welcoming and naming rituals, in the same way that Christians use water. For the Blood people of North America, the earth and the sun are important. An elder of the tribe marks the palm of his hand with red ochre and paints the sign of the tribe on the baby's face. Then he holds the baby up to the sun in the hope that its light will always shine on the child.

A MUSLIM BABY is prepared for its naming ceremony when it is a few days old by washing and shaving its head so that it is clean and ready to make a new start. The parents give thanks by donating money to those in need. It is traditional to give the same amount of silver as the weight of the baby's hair. A baby's hair does not weigh much, of course, so parents often give more than this.

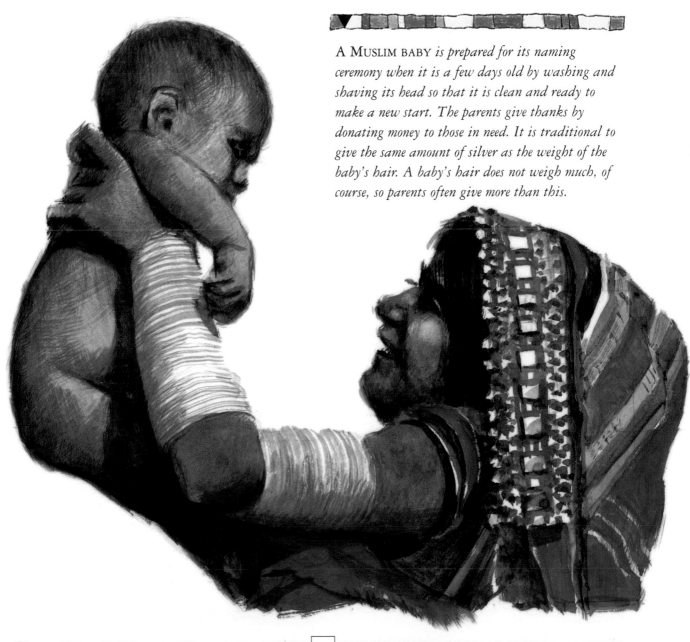

What's in a Name?

Parents choose names for their babies for many reasons. They may name a baby after a relation such as a grandparent, or after a celebrity or someone else they particularly admire. Some parents choose names that are fashionable at the time or name a baby after a character in a favourite book. Many parents simply choose a name they like.

But to some cultures, the choice of name is crucial to the baby's future well-being. Choose the wrong name and the consequences simply do not bear thinking about – the evil spirits will have a field day!

BALI IS THE *only island in the whole of Indonesia where the people are Hindus, rather than Muslims. Their dancers are world-famous.*

In Borneo, it was traditional not to name a baby for the first few years of its life as this would attract the attention of the evil spirits. And if a child went through a period of bad luck after he or she had been named, it was thought that the spirits had seen through the trick. The child was often renamed to throw the evil spirits off the scent again.

Sometimes, the stars the baby was born under are important considerations when choosing a name. The Aztecs of Mexico chose a baby's name by visiting an astrologer. The astrologer consulted a special book to see what the signs had been when the child was born. If there had been a storm, for example, this affected the name which the baby should be given.

In Myanmar (Burma), it is still the tradition to use astrological signs before coming to a decision. The days of the week each have letters allotted to them and children must have a name beginning with a relevant letter for their birth date.

In Bali, Indonesia, people must be called something that is completely unique to them. Since existing words are not unique, names are normally a jumble of nonsense words that mean nothing. These names are so personal that they are hardly ever spoken out loud and the holder of the name may be the only person who knows what it is. For everyday use, young people are normally known by a name which shows their place in the family, such as the first son. Adults are known by names which show their status in life.

Among the Navaho people of North America, the mother sometimes names daughters and the father names sons. But the mother can ask another close relative to choose a name. For example, she might ask a sister to name the child. The sister may give her own name or choose that of another relative. It is thought to be particularly good luck to give a child the name of someone who has lived for a long time.

A Jewish Naming Ceremony

In many cultures, boys and young men are circumcised as part or their naming or initiation ceremony. Circumcision is an operation during which the foreskin is removed from the penis. Jewish boys are circumcised as part of their naming ceremony, usually at eight days old.

The Jews are following the words in the Bible, from the book of Genesis, which say that 'every man child among you shall be circumcised'. In carrying out this operation, they are showing that the babies will lead good lives and follow God's laws.

In Europe and the United States of America, the ceremony usually takes place at home or in hospital. Some Jewish babies are circumcised in the synagogue. The boy is held by his godfather as the godfather, the rabbi and the other men present recite a greeting in Hebrew: 'Blessed be he that cometh.'

The godfather then sits down with the child on his knees and the circumcision takes place, while the people pray. The operation is traditionally performed by an official called a 'mohel', though nowadays it is more likely to be carried out by a doctor. After the circumcision, the child is given his name.

Adult men who become Jews must also be circumcised (this is almost always done in hospital) and receive a new name.

· Birth Customs · of the Navaho People

Among the Navaho people of North America, the birth of a baby took place in an earth–covered wooden cabin known as a 'hogan'. The pregnant woman had to take certain precautions to ensure that the birth was successful. She had to make sure that she did not tie any knots during her pregnancy as this could cause the baby to get tangled up with the umbilical cord. She was not allowed to turn the work on her loom upside-down in case the baby was born the wrong way round.

THE START OF LABOUR
When labour began, the mother drank some herbal tea. Her husband sprinkled sand on the floor and old cloths or a sheepskin were laid on the sand. The woman knelt on this covering, let her hair down and took off her jewellery. A red sash sprinkled with pollen was hung from the roof for her to hold during labour.

HASTENING THE BIRTH
If the labour was long, the other women let down their hair to help things along. The midwife also kneaded the mother's stomach, rubbed her with pollen and even held her upside-down which must have been a feat in itself. If all this did not help the baby to arrive, a singer might perform a song and beckon the baby out with an eagle-feather brush.

THE ARRIVAL OF THE BABY
For the birth, one woman knelt in front of the mother to hold the baby while another held the mother from behind. Sometimes the father pressed on the mother's stomach to push the baby out.

FIRST BATH
When the cord had been cut, the woman who had held the baby gave it its first bath. The child was then wrapped in a sheepskin or cloth and put next to its mother with its head towards the fire. Pollen was sprinkled on the baby's head as it lay there.

SHAPING THE BABY
The woman who had bathed the baby then 'moulded' the nose, head and limbs. This ritual ensured that the baby would grow into a healthy child with a straight nose and long, strong limbs.

A YEMINI MOTHER *and baby go into seclusion for forty days after the birth. The baby is wrapped in bands to re-create the security of the mother's womb.*

IN CAMEROON IN *West Africa, a new mother paints her face to ask for a blessing and protection from the spirits for her newborn child.*

Protecting the New Born

E ven after the baby was born, it was not safe from all the evil around it. In many societies, the midwife or doctor will put a new-born baby straight into its mother's arms to begin the 'bonding' process which is how a baby learns to know its mother.

However, the Akha tribe of Thailand would be horrified at such an idea. A new-born Akha baby must cry three times before anyone will touch it. The three cries are thought to be appeals to the god Apoe Miyeh for a soul, a blessing and a long life. When the baby has cried three times, it can be touched, but now it is at risk from the evil

spirits who think that a baby without a name is unwanted and therefore available for them to snatch away. So the midwife picks up the baby and gives it a temporary name as protection. The child is not given a proper name until later on when it has shown that it is healthy enough to survive.

The Chinese are even more pessimistic about a baby's chances of survival during the first few weeks, probably because many Chinese babies used to die at or soon after birth. The birth of a baby is not announced until a month later, to keep the spirits in the dark. Then the baby's Full Month Feast is held. Girls are given traditionally pretty names at this feast but boys are still in danger from

the spirits. They are given the name of an animal or a girl's name to fool the spirits into thinking that they are not worth harming. They do not receive their proper names until much later on, when they are deemed to be strong enough to cope with the responsibility.

In some Christian countries, there was a sneaking fear of evil spirits, goblins and malignant fairies, or 'little folk' who might steal the baby, as recently as the nineteenth century. Stories of changelings – fairies left instead of babies – are common. In Scotland, a mother and new-born child had to be introduced to the 'little folk' who lived in the

hearth. A lighted candle was carried three times round the bed where they lay. A Bible and a morsel of food were placed under her pillow as a gesture to ask God to protect mother and child. Sometimes, the child was put on to a cloth spread over a basket of food and carried three times round the crook of the chimney where the little folk lurked.

A Hindu baby's head is shaved when it is one year old because Hindus believe that a person goes through many lives. It is therefore important that the baby starts off on a good footing. Shaving the head removes any evil from the child's past lives.

Adoption Rituals

Sometimes women have babies which they cannot look after for one reason or another. They may feel that the baby would be better looked after by someone else and so they offer it for adoption.

Children who have been abandoned by their parents or whose parents have died may also be adopted. This means that someone else will bring up the child as their own. Perhaps a couple cannot have a child of their own and desperately want a baby. Adoption may be the ideal answer.

The main reason for adopting a child used to be the need for having a male heir to carry on the family line. If a couple did not have a son of their own, they adopted one. Often they were not too concerned about the child's welfare just so long as he bore their name.

Today, adoption laws have been tightened up in many societies to make it more difficult to adopt children. Careful checks are made to ensure that the couple who want to adopt can provide the child with a good home and education. The child may be brought up to believe that the adoptive parents are his or her natural parents, at least until he or she is old enough to understand what has happened.

Children who have been adopted are often curious about their natural parents. They need to know who they are so that they can

ADOPTION IN CHINA

In China, it is still important for a rich man to have a son who will carry on the male line and worship the spirits of his ancestors. If he did not have a natural son, the family would often adopt a boy.

CHOOSING AN HEIR
The man is expected to choose a member of his father's family. If there are no suitable heirs among his father's brothers or their sons, the man moves on to his grandfather's descendants, and so on until he finds someone who fits the bill. If the man can offer his heir a secure future, the boy's family will probably agree to the adoption. Adoption between brothers is fairly informal but adopting from more distant relations must be accompanied by a lavish banquet. All the elders sign a banner of red cloth to show that the adoption is legal.

RITUAL INSULTS
Sometimes a man is forced to adopt from outside his own family by buying an heir. When this happens, an even more lavish banquet is held, during which the guests taunt the father because he could not provide a son of his own. This is all part of the adoption ritual.

Couvade

A strange custom which is still practised among some cultures is known as 'couvade,' from the French word for 'brooding' or 'hatching'. The exact way in which this is practised varies from place to place but the general idea is for the father to go through the pregnancy with his wife, in some cases suffering even more than she does.

In some African tribes, the father takes to his bed as soon as his wife's pregnancy is announced and stays there until the baby is born. Meanwhile, the mother carries on with her everyday chores as the baby grows inside her. She does not stop working until a few hours before the baby is born.

So why do women allow their menfolk to languish in bed while they have to work and carry the baby? Because they believe that men are cleverer than them! The men are also physically stronger than the women and this combination of brains and strength makes the men better able to ward off evil spirits.

In Guyana, the mother worked hard until she gave birth and then went back to work immediately afterwards. The father had to stay in bed during what would normally be the mother's confinement. He was not allowed to eat certain foods, or to smoke, wash, or touch any of his tools or weapons. Only if he obeyed these rules would the baby be healthy.

However, even a man practising couvade cannot take the pain of birth from his wife. In medieval Europe, women tried to pass on the birth pains by donning their husbands' clothes as soon as they became pregnant. The idea was that if the woman took the man's place, perhaps the man would take hers.

SOME PEOPLES WHO *practise couvade do not go to such extremes. Some Pacific Islanders separate a husband and wife during the birth and for a few days afterwards. The man must stick to a special diet and not do anything seen as 'man's work'.*

Initiation

The age at which a person becomes an adult varies around the world. In some societies, people are regarded as adults as soon as they reach adolescence. In other places, they may have to wait until they are twenty or thirty years old. The rituals that mark a child's coming of age are known as 'initiation ceremonies'. In fact, any rites celebrating the beginning of a different stage in life can be called an 'initiation', which simply means the introduction of something new.

One of the biggest celebrations in many communities is the time when a child becomes an adult, or 'comes of age'. This may be a religious coming-of-age, or it may be more practical, when the young person is given the freedom to do whatever he or she likes, without having to seek parental permission. Along with this goes the responsibility the young adult must now take for his or her own life. No more can parents be relied on to provide money, a home, or to take the difficult decisions.

The coming-of-age ceremony can take many forms. In some societies, the young person has to go through an ordeal or undertake afeat of bravery. Some religions have special rituals which mark a person's move to adulthood. Or the occasion is marked by handing over a symbolic object., such as a front-door key

Even when someone has become an adult, there may be further initiation rituals. There are traditional rituals concerned with certain official or social occasions. Acceptance into a position of honour is normally accompanied by a special ceremony. Even entry into some professions is marked with rituals.

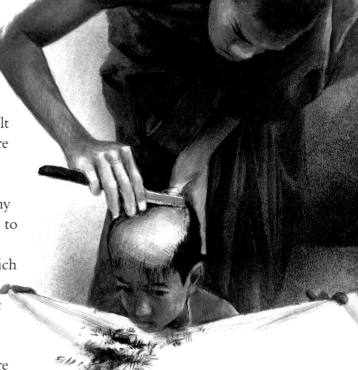

DEDICATION
In many cultures, a child's first haircut is a traditional sign of growing up. Here, a child's head is being shaved to mark the start of a period of study in a Buddhist monastery.

Going to School

A small child's first day at school can be a frightening experience. Suddenly the cosy, reassuring presence of the family is removed. He or she has to get used to obeying instructions, working in strange new surroundings and mixing with other people.

Most children also feel excited about going to school. If the school has a uniform, there is the fun of putting on all the new clothes for the first time. There is the prospect of making new friends, finding out new things and beginning to feel more 'grown up'. At many schools, children are formally welcomed by the head teacher and class teacher on their first day. Exchanging names with new people helps children to feel part of the new society.

All school initiations are not so pleasant, however. At some schools, older pupils tease newcomers with practical jokes. Tricks like making new pupils an apple-pie bed and sticking a hairbrush into it, or misleading pupils about rules so that they get into trouble have long been the tradition in boarding schools. This is a way of testing newcomers, and forcing them to prove themselves worthy of the respect of fellow pupils.

STARTING SCHOOL

Some cultures have special ways of marking the first big life change, starting school. These rituals are designed to acknowledge that the child is taking a big step in life, the first step on the path to becoming a self-sufficient adult.

COURAGE!
A Jewish tradition was to give a child a spoonful of honey before going to school for the first time. The sweet taste of the honey was a treat to make up for the worry about the new experience. The honey was also meant to suggest that learning was sweet.

WELCOME!
On their first day at school, Japanese children dress in their best clothes for a welcoming ceremony. This ritual is supposed to reassure the children and also to impress the importance of school on them. A group photograph is taken to mark the occasion.

Buddhism

Buddhists have fewer feasts and festivals than many other religions and there is no initiation ceremony except for people who want to become monks or nuns. Most of those entering Buddhist monasteries are boys – they must be at least eight years old before they can have a 'Pravrajya' ceremony which starts their life as a trainee monk.

In Burma, the Pravrajya is a grand occasion in which the boy acts out the story of Prince Siddhartha who gave up riches to seek enlightenment. The boy is dressed up like a prince and led through the town on a donkey, followed by a big procession of people. At the monastery, he asks the monks if he may join them. He takes off his elaborate clothes and puts on the simple orange robe of a monk. Then his head and eyebrows are shaved, and he vows to obey the Ten Precepts, or rules of good behaviour which he has learned.

Boys do not have to become monks for life. Often they enter a monastery for a few months before starting work. They learn that expensive possessions are not everything.

DRESSING FOR ADULTHOOD
Coming-of-age rituals often involve wearing special costumes. Here, a young Christian wears white to symbolize purity at her confirmation ceremony. The novice monk wears a white habit as a sign that he will lead a pure, good life in the Church. In some societies, the face is painted in various designs which have different meanings.

Hinduism

Hindus have an initiation ceremony called the 'Upanayana Samskara', which means the 'Rite of the Sacred Thread'. Only boys from the top three castes or classes of society can take part in this ceremony, which is held between the ages of eight and twelve. The castes are Brahmans (priests), Kshatriyas (warriors) and Vaisyas (traders and farmers).

The day for the ceremony is chosen by an astrologer who studies the stars and planets to find a lucky time. At the ceremony, the priest prays in front of the sacred fire, and then takes up the sacred thread which he has blessed. This is a length of white cotton cord which the priest loops over the boy's left shoulder and under his right arm.

The boy wears the thread as a sign that he has been reborn as a high-caste Hindu. In the past, Hindu boys studied with a guru for several years after they had been given their sacred thread. Today, it is more usual for them simply to learn a prayer from the priest at the initiation ceremony. Only boys and men who have had the Upanayana ceremony are allowed to know this prayer.

Graduation

At the end of the school year, many schools have a special assembly where the names of those who are leaving are read out. There may be a presentation of a gift such as a book. Schools linked to religious establishments often hold a special service to wish school-leavers good fortune.

At high schools in America, school-leavers celebrate with the high-school 'prom'. They dress up in formal clothes, long dresses for the girls and tuxedos for the boys, and go to an all-night party. Traditionally, this is the first time they are allowed to stay out all night with their parents' approval.

Every college and university has some form of award ceremony when students are officially given their degrees, and sent out into the world. Some of these ceremonies follow strict rituals which have been observed for years. Graduating students wear academic gowns for the first time. There can be formal processions with all the professors in their robes and hoods, and speeches in Latin or Greek!

THESE HUNGARIAN STUDENTS *are leaving school, ready to go into further education or find a job. Smartly dressed in formal dark suits, they carry bunches of flowers, which are good luck presents from parents, relatives and friends.*

Learning the Hard Way

Pity the student going to a German university in the fifteenth century. He had to dress up as an animal, with horns and large wooden teeth. The other students would then hunt him down, saw off the horns and pull out the teeth with pincers. His body was then smeared with a revolting ointment, and he was forced to eat pellets of cow dung.

A grain of salt was placed on his tongue to symbolize wisdom, and wine was poured on his head as a token of the happiness that his new wisdom would bring him.

STUDENTS AT AN *English university wear black gowns with hoods decorated in different colours or fabrics to show what type of degree they have been awarded. Parents and other relatives attend the graduation ceremony.*

Old School Tie

Throughout their lives people form associations which bind them together. This often begins during their schooldays. In Europe, and particularly in Britain, men who went to certain expensive, well-known schools are often proud of the fact, and want others to know it. They like to wear a badge of identification instantly recognizable to other members of their social group.

The most common form of identification is the 'old school tie'. Each school has a tie with its own distinctive design which pupils can wear after they have left and become 'old boys'. A man meeting another wearing the same old school tie has an immediate point of contact. He does not need a formal introduction. He can tell instantly where that man fits into society.

Special ties are also worn by members of military regiments and of exclusive clubs. The ties single out their wearers as part of a known social group. This grouping has led to the so-called 'old boy network', in which men from the same social groups will help each other out whenever they can. Anyone who tries to raise his standing by wearing a tie which he has no right to is despised.

The American equivalent of the 'old school tie' grouping is the male 'fraternities', or brotherhoods in colleges and universities. Students who want to become members of these select fraternities have to undergo initiation tests or dares, some of which are quite dangerous. They may have to collect an item from a place they are not allowed into, or put an object in a place which is difficult to reach such as the top of a steeple or tower, or perform some other feat which shows how brave and manly they are.

TIES THAT BIND

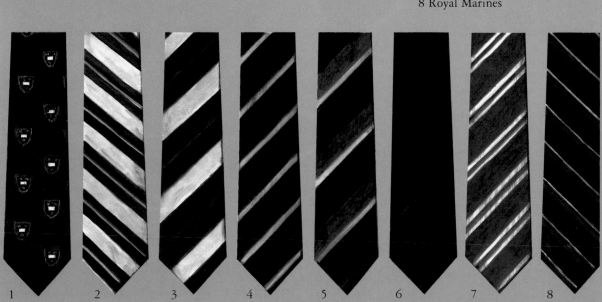

These are examples of special ties worn by members of British schools, universities, regiments and clubs. The right to wear such a tie shows that the person is a member of an exclusive and often privileged part of adult society.

1 Oxford University
2 Royal Scots Guards
3 Royal Gloucester Hussars
4 Old Etonians
5 Old Rugbyians
6 All England Lawn Tennis Club
7 Edinburgh University
8 Royal Marines

1 2 3 4 5 6 7 8

Bar Mitzvah

A Jewish boy officially becomes part of the adult community when he is thirteen years old. This is celebrated with a ceremony known as his 'Bar Mitzvah'. This is Hebrew for 'son of the Commandments', because Jews believe that when a boy is thirteen, he is old enough to understand and obey the Ten Commandments which God gave to Moses.

Jewish children study for a number of years before they are ready to take an adult place in the community. As well as learning the rituals used in the synagogue, they are taught Hebrew, the language of the Jews. For Jews who do not live in Israel, this is like learning a foreign language, but it is important because the 'Torah', the Jewish Bible, is written in Hebrew.

A boy's Bar Mitzvah ceremony is held in the synagogue on the first Saturday after his thirteenth birthday. He wears a prayer shawl for the first time and gives his first public reading from the Torah. At one time, it was customary for boys to give a lecture on Jewish religious laws to demonstrate what they had learned during their years of study. Nowadays, they are more likely to make a speech or say a prayer. The religious ceremony is followed by a party to which relatives and friends are invited.

After his Bar Mitzvah, a boy is regarded as an adult and a responsible member of the Jewish community and faith. He is eligible to make up the quorum needed for some Jewish ceremonies – especially important when the Jewish community is a small one.

In recent years, a similar ceremony for girls, the 'Bat Mitzvah', meaning 'daughter of the Commandments', has been introduced in some communities. A girl celebrates her Bat Mitzvah when she is twelve. The Bat Mitzvah takes a slightly different form from the boy's ceremony. Several girls usually take part in a joint ceremony in the synagogue.

Secret Societies

Some societies are not only exclusive, but very secret as well. No one knows exactly what goes on in these societies except the members themselves. These groups range from organizations such as the Freemasons to the so-called secret societies of traditional cultures, which are not secret in quite the same way (see page 43). But what is the point of these societies and what do they do?

THE SIGN OF *the Freemasons links the tools of their trade with more mystic symbols.*

The Freemasons is an all-male secret society which grew from the guilds of stone masons who built the castles and cathedrals of Europe in the Middle Ages. Members of the group, who are sometimes called 'Masons', claim that their motives are to encourage their members to do good works in society.

A man who is about to become a Freemason is taught a number of secret signs, passwords and handshakes with which he can make himself known to other Masons. He must keep these secret from anyone else.

His initiation ceremony takes place in a Freemasons' temple. Before he enters, he removes all his money, his watch and any other metal objects from his pockets. Then he is blindfolded and led into a windowless room lit only by candles, where the other members of the society are assembled. He is asked certain questions and has to get the

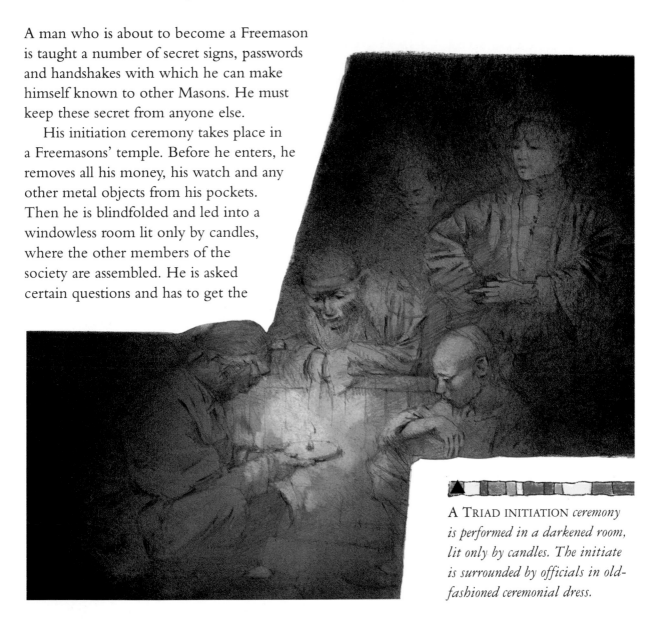

A TRIAD INITIATION *ceremony is performed in a darkened room, lit only by candles. The initiate is surrounded by officials in old-fashioned ceremonial dress.*

answers exactly right. Then, he has to go through various ordeals, still blindfolded, while the Masons bang together squares, compasses and other symbols of their trade.

At the end of this part of the ceremony, the words 'Let there be light' are spoken, and the initiate's blindfold is removed. He is now an apprentice Freemason. He is given a white lambskin apron, white gloves, and is introduced to the other Masons. As he moves up to higher grades within the Freemasons, he will have to take part in more initiation rituals.

Chinese secret societies such as the Triads have similar rituals. A Triad initiation

ceremony is performed in a place known as a walled city, palace or temple. The officials wear ceremonial costumes of the Ming dynasty, which began in the fourteenth century. The man being initiated is led into an inner courtyard known as the 'Red Flower Pavilion'. Here, he has to accept challenges and answer questions. He learns secrets of the society and swears an oath to tell no one else.

Men who join the Lions and similar societies such as the Elks, the Round Table and the Rotary Club, become part of a big international set-up. They wear special ties and have badges and car stickers showing that they are members of these groups.

• Initiation in New Guinea •

Initiation rituals among traditional cultures are often far more elaborate than those in the Western world. Most of the traditions go back hundreds of years and have scarcely changed during that time.

New Guinea, the second largest island in the world, lies in the south-west Pacific Ocean. The people of New Guinea have many complex rituals and ceremonies which involve special foods and costumes, the wearing of masks, dancing and the re-enactment of old legends. One example is the way in which the Gnau people celebrate the coming of age of their children. The rituals are similar for boys and girls, although there are some important differences.

At dawn on the day of the ceremony, girls wash with specially scented water. The guests begin to gather very early. If a child to be initiated is the family's first-born, relatives on the mother's side bring gifts. The traditional food of tubers mashed with coconut oil is cooked by the men.

Meanwhile, the mother cooks a special mixture of leaves and salt for the child to eat. Once the child has eaten this mixture, he or she may do certain things which are forbidden for children, such as smoking and chewing betel, a mixture of boiled dried seeds of the betel palm and the leaves of the betel pepper plant.

The next stage is to put the first part of a head-dress on the child. The men put the head-dress on the boy in their house, and then take him to a secret place away from the village for a special ceremony. During this ritual, some blood is a taken from a relative and dripped over the boy. Some of the blood is also mixed with the stew of tubers and coconut oil. Next, all the male relatives spit red betel juice at the child. A girl suffers this ordeal in public, but it is done in private

SORROWFUL STORY
Young boys perform a play about a group of children lost in the rainforest. This story is meant to demonstrate the sadness the initiates and their mothers feel about the end of their childhood.

for a boy. The sticky red juice is spread all over the child's body and allowed to dry.

Now comes the ritual meal which is an important part of the initiation. The stew is brought out in an earthenware pot, and spells are recited as it is eaten. If children are being initiated together, they eat the same stew and therefore become lifelong friends.

After the ritual meal, the child's head-dress is completed, and shell ornaments are given. Then, there is a big celebration feast, and the child is given gifts of money.

FRIGHTENING SIGHTS
The initiates must stay on their own inside the men's circular house. Every now and then, one of the elders enters the house wearing a terrifying mask. The young men are also forced to spend long periods without food or sleep, and to sit next to scorching fires for hours.

BOGEYMEN
Men rush around, choosing initiates to terrify even more. They are acting out the role of the ancestor spirits who will punish the young men if they do not behave themselves.

· Africa ·

The peoples of Africa have a variety of colourful customs for traditional initiation. Face and body paints and elaborate costumes are often worn and rituals may include shaving the initiates' heads and circumcision as well as feasting and dancing.

SAPANA WITH THE POKOTS OF KENYA

The coming-of-age ceremony of the Pokot people of Kenya is called 'sapana'. For a boy, the highlight of the festivity is when he is given his first mud cap, the sign of adulthood.

DRINKING

Initiates drink from a trough containing milk with a little ox blood. Oxen are very important to the Pokot, and their meat is always included at ceremonial feasts.

BLESSING

The boy is circumcised and spends some time alone. Then he is given a blessing before the first mud cap is applied.

HEADGEAR

The mud cap is put on carefully and then painted. It can only be worn in dry weather, when the mud bakes hard in the sun. Some Pokot men no longer use the mud cap as it breaks up in rain.

DISGUISING

Pokot girls also spend some weeks alone, their faces disguised with chalk.

DANCING

The young girls learn about their role in adult life during their weeks away from the community. When they emerge, they dance in a public ceremony to show that they are now adult women. The next step for most of them will be marriage.

BOY OR MAN?

The Masai people of East Africa have to wait for a mass celebration in their village, which happens every four or five years. A boy may be as young as thirteen or as old as seventeen when one of these celebrations is held. He must go through a series of rituals before he can become a 'moran' or warrior, and each step is of the utmost importance.

First, the boy's head is shaved, he takes a ritual bath and he is circumcised. He must not cry out during the operation, although his parents may wail for him. By undergoing this ordeal, the Masai boy has proved that he is manly and brave. He is now allowed to grow his hair again, and to dye his hair and body with red ochre. The boys in the group build their own houses in a special compound where they will live as the village's 'junior warriors'.

Meanwhile, the group who were initiated before them, now aged between twenty and twenty-five, move out of their compound and become fully-fledged members of the tribe who are allowed to marry. Their main task is to prepare the younger boys in the tribe for initiation. Later on, they will become elders.

For women in traditional societies, growing up means becoming a wife and mother, and much of their adolescence is spent learning about their future role in life. In Sierra Leone, young women are instructed on married life and then welcomed into the Bundu society at a special ceremony in the bush. A girl is not considered fit for marriage until she has been made a member of the Bundu.

AMONG THE POKOT *people, young women are ritually 'cicactrized' or scarred on the stomach and sometimes on the back and waist area, too.*

Cicatrization

This ritual inflicts cuts in the flesh in order to leave scars. It is a painful ordeal and is part of the initiation ceremony in various parts of Africa. Among the !Kung people of the Kalahari desert (in Namibia), after a boy has made his first kill, he undergoes a series of initiation ordeals. Cuts are made on various parts of his body and medicinal herbs are rubbed into the wounds to make his aim surer and his sight keener. Lastly he is presented with a new spear.

Australian Aboriginals

Many coming-of-age ceremonies have three main stages. First, the young person spends a period of time away from the group to demonstrate separation from the old life. Then the person is formally introduced to the new group. This stage is often accompanied by a period of learning and an ordeal of some kind. The final stage is the ceremony when the person officially becomes a member of the new group.

This pattern can be seen very clearly in the rituals practised by some Australian Aboriginals. First the boy dies and is reborn as an adult. Rituals symbolizing this process involve a young person becoming weaker and breaking links with his past life.

Then it is time to learn new things about being an adult. He is taught the myths surrounding the ancestors, and about the ceremonies and laws of his tribe. There is a painful physical ordeal such as circumcision or the removal of a tooth. This symbolizes the young person's return to society as an adult.

The ordeal may leave the person with a permanent scar which shows the world that he has been initiated, and separates him from children who have not. Or the initiate may be allowed to wear different clothes from before or paint his body in a special way.

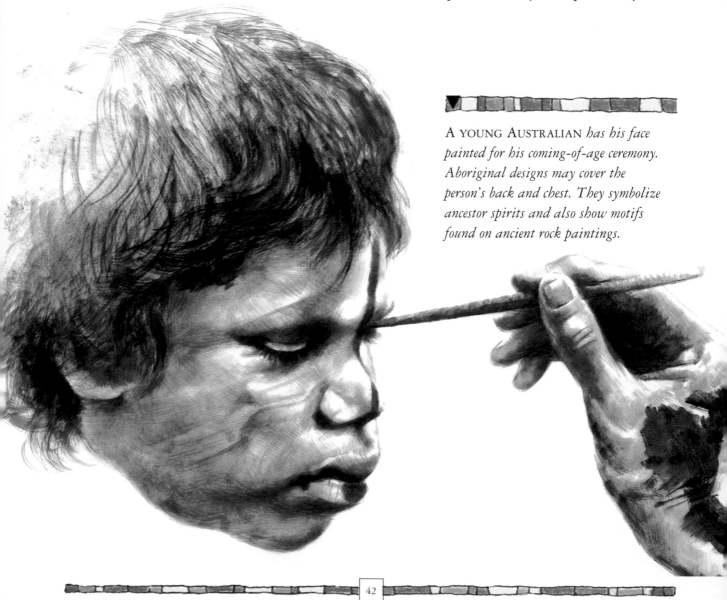

A YOUNG AUSTRALIAN *has his face painted for his coming-of-age ceremony. Aboriginal designs may cover the person's back and chest. They symbolize ancestor spirits and also show motifs found on ancient rock paintings.*

Traditional Secret Societies

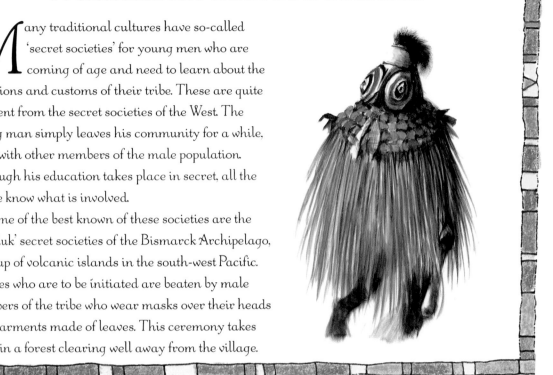

Many traditional cultures have so-called 'secret societies' for young men who are coming of age and need to learn about the traditions and customs of their tribe. These are quite different from the secret societies of the West. The young man simply leaves his community for a while, often with other members of the male population. Although his education takes place in secret, all the people know what is involved.

Some of the best known of these societies are the 'duk duk' secret societies of the Bismarck Archipelago, a group of volcanic islands in the south-west Pacific. Novices who are to be initiated are beaten by male members of the tribe who wear masks over their heads and garments made of leaves. This ceremony takes place in a forest clearing well away from the village.

FEMALE CIRCUMCISION

The circumcision of boys, in which the foreskin is removed from the penis, is carried out in some traditional societies during initiation ceremonies. It is also done to all Jewish baby boys when they are about eight days old, and in some Islamic societies, where young men are circumcised just before their marriage.

It is not known why or when circumcision first began, although it can have hygienic advantages because it is easier for the boy to wash himself properly. In western societies, where circumcision would not normally be carried out, boys can be circumcised on medical grounds because the foreskin is too tight.

There are no such advantages, however, to the circumcision of girls. This practice is not as widespread as for boys, but it is nevertheless practised by some traditional societies.

Female circumcision involves removing part of the sexual organs, so that the girl feels less pleasure during lovemaking. Often the girl, who is usually aged twelve to fifteen, is unaware of what is to happen and has not consented to it.

It has no purpose other than making the girl more obedient to her husband and less likely to succumb to the charms of possible lovers. It damages the girl's health because it can lead to kidney and bladder diseases, injury during lovemaking and difficulties in childbirth, and give the victim psychological problems.

There have been strong moves to end the practice of female circumcision, but they have met with little success. In the 1980s, it was estimated that more than 84,000,000 women in thirty countries had been circumcised.

•South America•

South American initiation ceremonies range from peaceful traditional rituals such as the Bemp celebration of the Kayapo people of Brazil to more violent and painful ordeals.

The Taulipang Indians of South America believe that a boy is not a man until he has been whipped, cut on the chin, arms and chest, and bitten all over by stinging ants. The whipping is to give the boy strength. The cuts on his chin are to make his aim with the blowpipe more accurate, while those on his arms make him better with his bow and arrow. The ants are put into a basketwork frame, pressed against his body and held there

BEMP – A CELEBRATION OF THE KAYAPO PEOPLE OF BRAZIL

This festival, which is held during the dry season, is named after a local fish. It includes rituals to celebrate coming-of-age, naming of children and marriage.

HEAD-DRESSES

The men wear elaborate head-dresses made of wax and feathers. The base is shaped from beeswax covered with feathers in vivid designs.

SYMBOLISM

The men keep an all-night vigil wearing their head-dresses. They believe that the first Kayapo climbed down from the sky on a rope. The shaft of the head-dress symbolizes this rope, and the feathers are the universe.

while they bite him all over. The agony keeps him lively, active and wide awake, making him an alert and energetic hunter.

Far from dreading the stinging ordeal and being glad when it is all over, the Taulipang regard the experience as a tonic to be repeated throughout life. If a man is feeling a little run-down or sluggish, he voluntarily suffers the ant treatment just to keep him on his toes. Not only does this help to ward off disease and pep up his hunting skills, claim the Taulipang, but it also improves a man's sense of humour!

Ants also play an important part in the lives of the Maue tribe. When a boy comes of age, he has to perform seven dances wearing a sleeve swarming with ants before he is regarded as a man.

Piercing the lower lip and wearing a lip plug is a symbol of manhood among Amazonian tribes. Lip piercing was also carried out by the early civilizations of Latin America, and symbolizes a man's strength as a warrior and talents as a speaker.

READY TO BE NAMED
This young boy is going to be given the name of an ancestor at a Bemp ceremony. His body is covered with soft yellow parrot feathers which are stuck on with glue. Pale blue eggshells are stuck to his head.

· North America ·

Coming-of-age is celebrated by all communities in North America, but the festivities are most colourful among the traditional societies. In the USA, young Americans consider themselves grown up when they can drive and own a car, so a coming-of-age ritual may involve handing over the keys of a new car, perhaps at a birthday party.

Among the Native Americans, traditions date back hundreds of years and include dances, costumes and ritual initiation ceremonies.

BEAT THAT!

Among the Zuni people of New Mexico, all young men are initiated into the Ko'tikili group. The young initiate has a sponsor, who is the husband, eldest son or eldest brother of the midwife who helped at his birth.

At the initiation ceremony, the sponsor leads the young man into his ceremonial house or 'kiva'. Two women put folded cloths on his back, and the sponsor wraps his head in a cloth so he cannot see. Then, four men, wearing masks to disguise them as gods, beat him with branches from the yucca plant. They beat him four times on his back, then they beat the women, and finally they beat the young man again.

After all this, the four 'gods' take off their masks so that everyone can see who they are. A 'god' hands each initiate a mask and yucca branch, and the initiates then beat the 'gods'. Finally, the 'gods' put their masks back on and beat the sponsors. So the young initiates become members of the Ko'tikili.

UP FROM THE UNDERWORLD

The Hopi Pueblo people of Arizona and New Mexico have four societies for men and three for women. These societies carry out rituals in their kivas, which are underground chambers. These have a raised part at the southern end and a sunken part at the northern end. Rituals are carried out at the northern end, which has a hole in the floor. This represents the hole through which the first Hopi climbed up from the underworld, according to their creation myth.

In one initiation ceremony, masked men represent the spirits who came up from the underworld with the first Hopi people, but had to return there. It is vital that the young initiates witness this ceremony, otherwise they cannot be sure of a place in the underworld when they die.

HOPI GIRLS

A Hopi girl cannot become a woman until she has spent four days by herself, grinding corn in the house of an aunt. If the girl gets an itch on her body or her head during this time, she is not allowed to scratch it with her hand but must use a stick. After her period of isolation, she emerges with a new hairstyle to show that she is a woman and ready to marry.

APACHE COMING OF AGE

In common with other Indian tribes, young Apaches become part of a 'totem group', which is a group of people who all have the same mythical ancestor, often an animal. Here, a young Apache woman follows a ritual that will bring her closer to her ancestor spirit at her coming-of-age ceremony. The dances are to attract good spirits and ward off evil forces.

SPONSORSHIP
Each child who is coming of age has a 'sponsor', often a relation or someone who has a special relationship with the initiate. The sponsor's role is to help the initiate at the ceremony.

Here, the young woman's father presents the sponsor with a feather. By taking the feather, she accepts this role.

DANCING
The young woman kneels on a pad of buckskin to perform her ritual dances. She is directed by her father, who holds her sacred cane, and by her sponsor, who holds two eagle feathers.

RUNNING
The young woman runs around her sacred cane. She must go fast so that no evil can catch her.

YELLOW SHOWER
She is sprinkled with yellow cattail pollen. This pollen is a holy substance to the Apache.

THE FINAL DANCE
The young woman is painted all over for the final stage of the ceremony. She is blessed from four sides in turn, and then takes part in a dance around the frame of a tepee.

Promotions and Honours

Initiation rituals are not just concerned with coming of age, as we have already seen. When a person accepts a position that means an important life change, there is often a ceremony. Promotion at work often means taking on more responsibility and a pay rise. The occasion may simply be marked by a drink or going out for a special meal.

Sometimes a person's achievements are regarded highly enough to grant them a special honour. This may take the form of a medal or a special presentation of some kind. The person may receive a new title that sets him or her apart from other people.

The rituals for presenting honours date back hundreds of years. A candidate who is to receive a knighthood, for example, kneels before the monarch on a low velvet stool. The monarch touches each of his shoulders with the flat of a sword blade and bids the new knight to rise. This ritual dates back to medieval times, when young men spent years working their way up through the ranks in the courts of Europe. Today, knights are people who have performed a special service for the community, rather than brave warriors, but the ritual for conferring the honour has hardly changed. The knight may also receive a medal or some special insignia which the monarch pins to his coat or hangs around his neck on a ribbon.

Other rituals for giving honours are more straightforward, perhaps involving pinning a medal on to a coat or uniform, or handing over some special certificate. Sometimes the person receiving the honour has to make a promise or take an oath. New members of parliament usually take their seats during a formal ceremony. During this they swear an oath of allegiance, promising to serve the country faithfully and abide by its laws.

MAKING A KING OR QUEEN

The more important the person being initiated is, the more elaborate the ceremonies become. At the top of the list are the celebrations and ceremonies which are staged when a new ruler is appointed.

If that ruler is a king or a queen, there will be a coronation like the crowning of the British queen, Elizabeth II, in 1953.

CORONATION

Queen Elizabeth II was crowned in one of Britain's great churches, Westminster Abbey in London. Everyone in the ceremony wore elaborate robes of office or uniforms to show their rank. The highest ranking Anglican priest, the Archbishop of Canterbury, presided over the ceremony.

He spoke the words 'I here present unto you Queen Elizabeth, your undoubted Queen...' which gave the assembled people a chance to acknowledge the new queen and show her their loyalty.

Then the new monarch was anointed to show her spiritual role as leader of the Anglican Church. Next she was presented with the

Sword of State as a symbol of her power as Britain's military leader. Finally the weighty St Edward's Crown was placed on her head, and she was presented with the Sceptre with the Cross, symbolizing power and justice, and the Rod with the Dove, representing equality and mercy for her people.

Marriage

A wedding ceremony is a great occasion, probably one of the most important in an adult's life. For months beforehand, the bride and groom prepare for their big day. The wedding dress must be bought or made. A guest list is drawn up and plans are made for the ceremony itself and the celebrations afterwards.

There are many different styles of wedding ceremony around the world. Most of them are steeped in ancient customs and rituals. A marriage may be a religious ceremony, but it does not have to be. Some marriages are very simple. The couple may just take their marriage vows with two friends to act as witnesses. Other weddings are very elaborate with hundreds of guests, and celebrations lasting for hours or even days.

The clothes worn by the bride and groom are usually traditional and range from a white dress and veil, symbols of purity, for the Western bride, to the elaborate face paints and head-dresses of other societies. It is customary for an English bride to dress in new clothes from head to foot for the wedding. This stems from the old tradition that a husband should not have to inherit any of his wife's debts. The bride's new clothes symbolize her fresh start in life.

Many marriage rituals are connected with the symbolic handing over of the bride to her new family. In some cultures, the bride arrives at the wedding with her father or whoever is 'giving her away' to her new husband. Or she may be led to the ceremony in a procession, accompanied by musicians, priests and members of her family.

Some rituals are rather more dramatic. In New Guinea, for example, women from the bride's family stage a mock battle to stop her leaving her group. The women dress in warrior-style clothing for this battle, with feather head-dresses and paint on their faces.

After the wedding ceremony, there is

Buddhist Nuns

Many Buddhist boys become monks, but far fewer Buddhist girls become nuns. This is because Buddhists frown on the idea of a girl giving up the responsibilities of marrying and bringing up a family.

Some girls do brave disapproval and become nuns. They either live in a convent or share a monastery with monks, although they have their own separate living quarters.

Buddhist nuns wear the same orange robes as monks and are expected to lead the same simple life.

usually a celebration. This may be a party where all the guests gather together to congratulate the newly-married couple and drink a toast to their future happiness, or it may be a more elaborate ritual with singing, dancing and the acting out of mock battles between the sexes. But whatever happens, it is always a happy occasion when people dress up to join in the celebrations and help the couple to start the marriage off in style.

BRIDE OF CHRIST

When we think of a wedding, we automatically imagine a man and a woman getting married. But another type of marriage is performed when a woman decides to become a nun. In the Christian Church, a nun is known as a 'bride of Christ' because she has vowed never to marry a man, but to wed herself to the Church instead. She lives in a convent with other nuns, and devotes her life to God. Some nuns lead a life of prayer and contemplation. Others tend the sick or run schools in developing countries.

When a woman becomes a nun, she gives up all her possessions, clothes and jewellery. While she is in the convent, she wears the traditional 'habit,' or clothes of a nun.

Women do not always have to give up the idea of marriage when they become nuns. In India, a girl will sometimes make a symbolic marriage to one of the Hindu gods, but she would be free to marry later on if she wants to.

• What to Wear •

Most cultures have traditional clothes for a wedding. These garments make the bride and groom stand out from the crowd, and may also have a symbolic significance, like the white dress of the Western bride. In some cultures, there are also special clothes for courtship rituals.

▼ MEXICO

At country weddings in Mexico, the bride is hidden behind a thick white veil until halfway through the ceremony. Both bride and groom wear white. Mexico is a Roman Catholic country, so the bride and groom wear rosaries and crucifixes which are heirlooms of both families.

▼ YEMEN

The women of both families help to decorate the face of a Yemeni bride for her wedding. She wears long elaborate earrings as a sign of prosperity.

KAZAKHSTAN ▶

In Kazakhstan, which used to be part of the USSR, people wear traditional cone-shaped hats for weddings and other celebrations. Today, these are mainly worn by Muslims.

▼ MOROCCO

A royal bride in Marrakesh wears layers of robes and head-dresses that take hours to put on. Once dressed, she can hardly move and has to sit on a cushion for the whole marriage ceremony, which lasts for three hours.

▲ JAPAN

This Japanese bride wears the traditional dress of a kimono and cone-shaped head-dress with a veil, while the groom wears a Western-style dark suit.

▲ ECUADOR

The groom holds a lighted candle throughout the marriage ceremony. Its flame is a symbol of the couple's everlasting love for each other.

▲▲ NIGER

This Fulani man from Niger hopes to attract a wife at the festival of Geerewol. He paints his face and decorates his hair with beads and shells.

◀ WESTERN EUROPE

The traditional clothes for European and American weddings are a white dress and veil for the bride and a formal suit for the groom. English and American brides add 'something old, something new, something borrowed and something blue' for luck. 'Something old' is in memory of past happiness, while 'something new' is a symbol of the new marriage. 'Something borrowed' is for the loyalty of the bride's friends who lend her their support. Blue is the colour for faithfulness, so 'something blue' shows that she will be true to her husband.

Tying the Knot

Marriage ceremonies take many forms and the only stipulation is that they must be legally binding. In many countries, people can choose a religious ceremony or a civil one and both count as an official marriage. At a civil ceremony, the couple are married by an official in a registry office or Town Hall. In France, however, the only legal form of marriage is a civil ceremony at the Town Hall. Couples can choose to have a religious ceremony as well.

All religions have a form of marriage ceremony. Some ceremonies are conducted in a place of worship, but this is not always the case. Buddhist weddings usually take place in a hall or a hotel, although the couple are married by monks. The bride and groom both wear silk clothes and sit on silk cushions in front of the monks. During the marriage, a silk scarf is wrapped around their hands to tie them together, and they eat from the same silver bowl as a sign that they will share things in their future life. After the service, the couple may go to a local temple to have their marriage blessed by the monks.

Most Muslim weddings take place at the bride's home. Unlike most other weddings, the bride and groom do not actually see each other until after the ceremony. They sit in separate rooms in the house, the bride with the female guests, and the groom with the men. An 'Imam', a Muslim holy man, usually conducts the service, asking the bride if she wants to marry the groom, and then presenting the groom with the wedding contract to sign. When the formalities have been completed, all the guests recite from the 'Qur'an', the holy book of Islam, and pray for the happy couple.

THE RITUALS IN *a marriage ceremony are often long and elaborate. The marriage itself is a solemn occasion, as the couple make their vows to each other. But afterwards there is dancing and merrymaking to celebrate the occasion.*

A COUPLE TAKE *their marriage vows in front of a priest. They promise to love and honour each other, no matter what life may bring.*

ring on the first finger of the bride's left hand. He tells everyone that she is now his wife, and then he moves the ring to the third finger. At the end of the marriage ceremony, the groom breaks a small glass with his foot, and the guests shout 'Mazelt tov', which means 'congratulations'.

The 'Evil Eye' is Watching You

In some cultures, people worry that the 'Evil Eye' will ruin everything at a wedding. So this is another time for elaborate precautions to fool the spirits into thinking that nothing out of the ordinary is going on.

The wedding veil, a symbol of purity today, was once a disguise against the 'Evil Eye'. The bride was hidden under the veil so the spirits could not see her until she was safely linked with her husband. In Morocco, a bride must keep her eyes shut throughout the ceremony to avoid the 'Evil Eye'.

In China, a bride is thought to be at greatest risk during the journey from her house to the wedding ceremony, which is usually held at the home of the bridegroom. So she travels in a closed sedan chair, hidden from view. A particularly cautious bride will sit in a box inside the chair!

Another way to fend off evil spirits is by using a 'false bride'. In Estonia on the Baltic Sea, formerly part of the USSR, the bride's brother often stands in for her – much to the confusion of all concerned.

In northern India, the groom sometimes marries a tree. While the evil spirits are busy attacking the tree, the groom then slips away quietly and marries his true bride.

Then, everyone gets together for a feast provided by the bride's family.

Most Jewish couples are married on a Sunday, and the wedding takes place in the synagogue. The couple stand together under a 'chuppah', a canopy which is a symbol of their future home and happiness. They drink from a cup of wine, and the groom places a

Christian Weddings

Most Christian weddings take place in a church, although couples can be married anywhere, so long as the ceremony is conducted by a priest or someone else who is officially entitled to carry out the formalities.

There are three main branches of the Christian Church – Protestant, Roman Catholic and Eastern Orthodox. At a Protestant wedding, the groom arrives at the church with his best man, usually a close friend or relation, who takes care of some of the arrangements. The bride traditionally arrives a few minutes late, just to keep everyone guessing whether she will turn up or not. She comes up the aisle on the arm of her father or whoever is giving her away, and is often followed by bridesmaids and pages.

During the ceremony, the couple make their marriage vows and exchange wedding rings. Afterwards, they sign the register which is the official record of their marriage.

Setting off on the Right Foot

A Western bride may not hide in a box for her journey to the church, but there are customs and traditions about her departure to her new life. First, she must step out of her house on the right foot, because it is bad luck to step out on the left foot. If the sun shines on the journey, that is good luck, but rain is a bad omen, unless the bride sees a rainbow on the way. If she meets a chimney sweep or an elephant, she can go to her wedding with a glad heart. A black cat is a more likely good luck symbol. But woe betide the bride who comes face to face with a pig en route, for that is a sign of bad luck.

WEDDING RINGS ARE *exchanged nowadays as a symbol of love and commitment. But, in ancient times, women wore wedding rings to show that they were the husband's property.*

The Eastern Orthodox branch of Christianity developed after the collapse of the Roman Empire in the fourth century AD. From Constantinople (now Istanbul in Turkey), the Eastern Orthodox religion spread through Eastern Europe, the Near East and Russia, where it is still practised today.

In Eastern Orthodox weddings, the bride and groom are both led into the church by their fathers, and the marriage takes place in front of the icon screen, a barrier which separates the altar from the main part of the church. The couple exchange rings and silver crowns which are blessed by the priest.

A WEDDING IN FRANCE

France is a country with strong Roman Catholic traditions. Although couples have to be married at the town hall for the wedding to be legal, many couples choose to have a religious ceremony as well. The wedding shown here is taking place in Burgundy, a region in eastern France, but similar ceremonies can be seen in other parts of the country.

BEFORE THE TRICOLOR
The wedding party gathers at the town hall for the civil ceremony which is conducted by the mayor, against the background of the tricolor, the French flag.

PROCESSION
After the civil ceremony, the bride, groom and their parents lead the guests in a procession to the church. The wedding is very public as passers-by stop to watch. The procession used to go on foot, but nowadays the guests often travel in a convoy of cars with horns blowing.

BEFORE GOD
In church, the couple exchange vows, the congregation prays and sings hymns, and the priest gives a short talk about marriage. The couple are now married in the eyes of the Church.

CONGRATULATIONS
After the wedding, the guests gather outside the church to congratulate the couple. Then everyone goes to a public hall for the 'vin d'honneur', a drinks party to which the whole community is invited. This is an opportunity for everyone to wish the couple good luck.

FEAST
The wedding guests then form another procession to go to the home of the bride or the groom, where a lavish feast has been prepared. Afterwards, there are speeches and toasts, and then the couple lead the guests in a dance.

• Weddings in India •

The Hindu religion is one of the world's most ancient. It began in India about 4,000 years ago, and is still practised by many millions of people. Hindus believe in many gods, and have some of the most elaborate and complex festivals of any religion.

The exact form that a Hindu wedding takes depends upon the caste (or class) of the people getting married and the part of India they live in. The country wedding shown here is a good example of one marriage rite.

Before the wedding itself, the groom travels to the bride's house in a procession, accompanied by musicians and crowds of friends and relations. Some walk, but the groom and close relatives travel on decorated bullock carts.

The groom is received as an honoured guest by the bride's parents. Gifts are exchanged and in higher-caste families, the bride's parents may give large sums of money to the groom's family.

PREPARATIONS ▶
The bride dresses in a red sari and wears gold jewellery. She paints her face carefully, and female relatives paint patterns on her hands and feet with red henna dye.

A Sikh Wedding

The Sikh religion was founded in India during the sixteenth century. It follows the teachings of its founder, Guru Nanak, and the nine gurus who followed him. The last of these, Guru Gobind Singh, said that after his death there should be no more gurus. Instead, every Sikh should follow the holy book, the 'Guru Granth Sahib', which would be their new leader. So there are no Sikh priests, and any Sikh can conduct religious ceremonies.

A Sikh bride wears a red sari or tunic and trousers, and her feet and hands are painted with henna, like a Hindu bride. The bride

HINDUS SET GREAT store by astrological predictions, so the families will consult the local astrologer before going ahead. They ask if their child has made a good choice of partner and to pick the wedding date.

and groom both wear long scarves. The service takes place in a Sikh temple or 'Gurdwara'. The couple sit in front of the holy book, while the Sikh idea of marriage is explained to them by the person who is conducting the ceremony. Then the couple bow to the Guru Granth Sahib to show that they agree to the marriage, and their scarves are tied together. They walk around the holy book while the guests sing hymns. After the service, there is a celebration meal.

THE WEDDING CEREMONY

*The ceremony is held outdoors,
either in a special marriage booth or
in a courtyard of the bride's house. A fire is lit in a metal
container. Everyone recites verses in Sanskrit, the ancient language of the Hindus, and
the couple throw rice into the fire. The bride's sari and the groom's long shirt are
knotted together to show that they are joined in marriage. The groom takes the bride by
the hand and leads her round the fire seven times as a symbol of their journey through
life together. Finally the couple make promises to each other and to the gods. After the
ceremony, there is a feast during which professional dancers may perform.*

Mind the Step!

Several societies have superstitions about crossing the threshold after marriage. The threshold, or entrance to the house, is supposed to be an unlucky place where evil spirits lurk, and it is traditional in the West for the husband to carry his bride over this dangerous place when they first enter their new home. However, another reason for the tradition may be that the bride could trip on the step and fall into her new home in an undignified manner.

The Journey Home

After the Hindu wedding, the bride and groom go to their new home in another procession. The bride must enter her home without crossing the threshold.

In some parts of India, girls marry when they are still children. A child bride goes to her husband's home for three days after the wedding, then returns to her family until she is old enough to live with her husband.

Arranged Marriages

In modern Western societies, people choose who they are going to marry, and they would not be too keen on any other way of doing things. But it used to be the custom, especially among rich and aristocratic families, for parents to choose a marriage partner for their child to make sure that he or she 'made a good match'. If a man or woman could bring a title, money or land into the marriage, this would please the parents, even if the couple hated the sight of each other.

Marriages are still arranged in many societies today. Sometimes a professional matchmaker is used to make the match. Japan has now adopted many Western customs, including allowing people to choose their own marriage partners, but arranged marriages used to be the norm. A go-between was employed to carry out the

THE BERBER FESTIVAL OF BRIDES

Morocco is a Muslim country but many people still carry out traditions which date back to pre-Islamic times. One of these is the Festival of Brides which is celebrated by the Ait Hadiddou people of the Atlas Mountains every September.

The aim is for men and women to choose a likely partner and get married, all within a few days. The marriages are arranged very quickly, but divorce can follow just as speedily. Many of the men and women at the festival are on the look-out for a new partner after a divorce.

ARRIVALS

Thousands of people come to the festival which is a good time for trading as well as arranging marriages.

Men who are looking for a wife wear white clothes so that they stand out, and a white turban with a square of cloth hanging down behind.

PREPARATIONS

The women wear a veil and a head-dress decorated with silver discs and glass beads. Their faces are almost completely hidden, and their bodies are wrapped in a woollen cape. The men have little chance of seeing what the women look like. Widows and divorced women wear pointed head-dresses.

negotiations around a formal meeting table. During these discussions, there was a ceremony known as 'mi ai', or mutual seeing, when the couple were allowed to see each other. If they liked the look of each other, the plans could go ahead. If not, the go-between was sent away to look for another partner.

Most Muslim marriages are arranged by parents who make suggestions to their son or daughter about a suitable partner. When a wedding is agreed on, the two families will exchange presents as a sign of good faith. In Saudi Arabia, a marriage between cousins is highly favoured because it strengthens the extended family. However, the final decision is left to the woman. If she says no, the wedding is off.

In Madagascar, a go-between chooses a likely wife for a particular man. The woman then has to stand in a group with other young women so that the man can go through a ritual of choosing his bride.

ENCOUNTERS
Groups of men and women watch each other as they stand and chat. The women are so well hidden that they can have a good look at the men without being seen.

After a while, men and women take the plunge and begin to talk, egged on by their friends and relatives. Then, some of them will pair off and make up their minds to get married.

MAKING IT OFFICIAL
If they decide to go ahead, they go to an official scribe who writes out a marriage application in Arabic. When the written applications have been prepared, the couples line up outside the tent of the 'qadi', an official of the Minister of Justice.

If the application is in order, the marriage is agreed by the qadi. The groom pays a fee to the government, and gives his wife some money. A woman who is divorced or widowed leaves with her husband and goes back to his village. A woman who has married for the first time returns to her own village and joins her husband later in the year.

•African Courtship and Marriage•

S ome of the most colourful weddings are held among the traditional societies of Africa. The festivities may last for several days and include wild, lively dancing, music, singing and ritual fights. People wear brightly coloured traditional costumes, often with elaborate head-dresses and sometimes with masks or face paints.

Dancing forms an important part of most traditional African celebrations, including courtship. The young Watusi women of Zaire carry out an elegant ritual dance to attract a husband. They imitate the graceful movements of the crane, as they advance and retreat with their outstretched arms waving slowly like the bird's wings.

The young men of the Wodaabe people who live in Niger put on an equally impressive courtship dance. The men from one clan or family group put on flowing robes and make their faces up carefully, paying particular attention to their eyes. Then, they circle around, singing and dancing as the women from other clans stand around and watch them. Eye contact is the key to this ritual. If one of the men catches the eye of a woman, this may be enough to start their courtship. In another ritual, the men roll their heavily made-up eyes to attract a partner.

BRIDE IN A BOX

Most people want to shout it from the rooftops when they get married but they will normally content themselves with putting an announcement in a newspaper. But a tradition among North African brides was far more showy. After the wedding, the bride was put into a wooden cage and paraded through the streets. A large group of musicians, friends, relations and anyone else who was interested, followed her in a procession, which usually took place by moonlight. Other people would shout good wishes from their doorways.

FAREWELLS
The princess is given a send-off by her friends and female relations in Swaziland. She bids a formal farewell to her family by dancing with her attendants, her breasts bare as a sign of her humility. The sleeping mat and gourd in front of the dancers represent the house that the princess is moving to. She holds a knife and two traditional spears called 'assegais' to show that she is going to join another clan. An ox's gall bladder is tied to her head as a token of good fortune.

A ROYAL WEDDING

In 1977, a princess from Swaziland married the king of the Zulu people of South Africa. Like all royal weddings, the ceremony was conducted in great style. There was loud music and vigorous dancing, colourful costumes, a mock battle and the presentation of gifts between both families. The people of Swaziland and the Zulus had been bitter enemies during the nineteenth century, and many of the wedding rituals illustrated their past battles and the fact that they had now come together in friendship.

THE PRINCESS APPEARS
The princess made a grand entrance, sweeping into the royal enclosure behind her warriors. Dancers and musicians surrounded the princess as she joined the king, who wore a cloak of leopardskin and a necklace of lion claws. Then, the bride and groom took their vows.

THE PRINCESS PREPARES
The princess took a ritual bath and her body was covered with ox-gall. Then she dressed for the wedding. She wore a head-dress of feathers, and carried a sword, both symbols of her royal blood.

WAR AND PEACE
The wedding was held at the home of the Zulu king. Swazi warriors who had accompanied the princess on her journey staged a mock battle with their Zulu hosts as part of the celebration.

This was a reminder of the time when the two peoples were at war, and also prepared everyone for the princess's grand entrance.

DANCING AND GIFT-GIVING
After the marriage ceremony, everyone joined in a celebration dance. The bride's father had already given cattle to the Zulu king. Now the princess gave presents to her new family. Dozens of the king's relatives sat waiting for their gifts of sleeping mats, blankets and bowls.

• The Wedding Feast •

Most weddings are followed by a special meal of some kind. This often takes the form of a feast or reception where guests gather to eat, drink and congratulate the newly-married couple. There may be speeches and people often drink a toast to the bride and groom, the families involved and the bridesmaids.

Some of the foods served at wedding feasts are symbolic. Before the days of refrigerated ships and faster transport, people had to rely on foods which could be grown locally, and many traditional wedding foods reflect this.

In Poland, for example, the staple crop is wheat, and so a special plaited loaf of bread called a 'kolacze' is traditionally served at a Polish wedding feast. Good, simple food is served at the feast, including some meat, peas and gravy, and 'borscht' soup which is made from beetroot. When the guests have been served, they all cry 'The soup is bitter', until the bride and groom kiss each other. There is always plenty of food as a symbol that the couple will not have to go without during their married life.

In The Netherlands, a newly-married couple used to be given a mixture made from salted cream sprinkled with sugar. This represented the bitter and sweet sides of married life.

A Good Send-off

It is traditional in some societies for the bride and groom to leave the wedding reception while the party is still in full swing. The guests gather to see them off as they drive away to start their new life. In many countries, guests throw confetti or rice over the couple as they leave, a tradition which may annoy the people who have to sweep up afterwards, but does not do any more damage than that.

In Anglo-Saxon times, however, the send-off was rather more violent. During the ceremony, the bride's father gave the groom one of his daughter's shoes as a sign that he was handing her over to her new owner. The groom then banged the bride over the head with the shoe to show her who was boss. Then the bride's parents threw an old shoe at the poor girl to show that they had washed their hands of her.

FEASTS AROUND THE WORLD

This picture, in the style of the painting The Wedding Feast *by the Flemish painter, Pieter Bruegel, shows some of the traditional ways in which people celebrate a marriage. Offering food is a sign of hospitality, and one family, often the bride's, may provide the wedding feast as a gift to their new in-laws and friends and relations from both sides. The feast is also a good opportunity for the couple to have a party before they settle down to everyday living.*

▼ TOGETHERNESS

A couple from the island of Java eat food from each other's plates as a symbol of the sharing they will be doing in the future. Mixing white and yellow rice together is also part of the Javanese ceremony.

STUFF OF LIFE

The Ukraine is a farming country where wheat is the main crop, so an elaborately decorated loaf is included in the feast to remind the couple where most of their food will come from.

◄ LARGESSE

Even people who are poor lay on as big a display of food as they can manage to show the true meaning of hospitality. Here, a Romanian couple have laid out the food all over the floor and furniture.

·Dancing at the Wedding·

When the feast is over, it is the custom in many societies for the guests to get up and dance. The dance may be a traditional display in national costume or a ritual acting out of some historic occasion. At many weddings, the dancing is more informal. The bride and groom get up and start the dancing, and the other guests gradually join them.

DANCE OF THE WODAABE MEN
Dancing is a way of bringing people together in many societies. The dance may be in the informal style of most Western parties and discos, or it may be more formal, like the courtship dance of the Wodaabe men of Niger. As the men circle round, they hope to catch the eye of one of the women who are standing watching.

OLD AND YOUNG
Old and young can join together in dancing at a wedding.

DANCE OF THE CZECH
MARRIED WOMEN
*A Czech bride's female married relatives
perform a traditional dance of honour
for the bride. These women are dressed
in their national costume which is now
only worn for special celebrations.*

DANCE OF THE
CAJUN WOMEN
*In the city of New Orleans
in the USA, the
sisters of the bride
and groom perform
a dance that is
supposed to make
fun of their
unmarried status. They
stand on washtubs and wave
brooms decorated with ribbons,
as the guests look on, cheering
in delight.*

•Marriage in the Far East•

Marriage ceremonies in China, Japan, Malaysia and other countries in the Far East may follow the customs of one religion or take in aspects from several. In China, people may be followers of Buddhism, Taoism or Confucianism, but, since all the religions are relevant to their lives in different ways, people sometimes belong to all three. The tradition of ancestor worship is important in China, no matter which religion a person follows – this is reflected in the marriage ceremonies.

GO-BETWEENS AND ASTROLOGERS

A Chinese marriage is arranged by a go-between who is sent to the bride's house with a gift from the bridegroom. If the bride's family accepts the gift, the couple's horoscopes by the astrologers are checked to make sure that they suit one another. Then, the gods and spirits are consulted and asked to bless the couple and also to suggest a suitable day for the wedding.

The ceremony usually takes place at the bridegroom's house. Some brides and grooms wear elaborate silk clothes, decorated with good luck emblems such as dragons, although nowadays the groom often wears a dark suit instead. Gifts and prayers are offered to the gods during the wedding so that they will look kindly on the couple in the future.

HINDU AND ISLAM

Malaysia was once a Hindu country, but its main religion is now Islam. A Malaysian couple will therefore have a Muslim marriage ceremony, but Hindu traditions are often included. One of these Hindu customs is to treat the bride and groom like royalty on their wedding day.

EASTERN AND WESTERN DRESS

It is now customary for Japanese brides to wear a white wedding dress, like a Western bride. However, the bride may still wear a traditional kimono for some parts of the ceremony and a wedding dress for other parts.

• Providing a Dowry •

Until quite recently, it was normal practice for money or possessions to change hands as part of a marriage agreement, and this is still the custom in many societies, particularly when marriages are arranged. This idea goes back at least five thousand years.

Babylonian law stated that a wife had to bring property to the marriage with her, so making a contribution towards supporting her new family. In Western societies, the main point of 'making a good match' among the rich was to link fortunes or neighbouring tracts of land. If a landowner with an unmarried son lived next to a landowner with an unmarried daughter a marriage was a useful way of joining up parts of the land.

There are two types of marriage payment. One is a 'dowry', which is money or property the bride gives to her husband. The other payment is a 'bride-price' or 'bridewealth', which the husband pays to the bride's family to make up for the loss of their daughter. This is still common among some traditional African societies. Muslim bridegrooms pay money to the bride's family, but this becomes the bride's property when they are married. In China, the bride's family is given money as they are losing a daughter.

The dowry system has been forbidden in many places because of the trouble it has caused. In India, the dowry system was legally abolished in the 1960s, but wives are still ill-treated and even burned to death, if their families can not pay a dowry in full.

IF THE PRICE IS RIGHT

In many cultures, a woman's marriage prospects depend entirely on whether her parents can provide a substantial dowry. No money, no marriage is the rule. Similarly, if a man's family cannot afford the bride-price demanded by the family, then the wedding is off.

SYMBOL OF VALUE
The Surma women of Ethiopia put a wooden or earthenware plate into their lower lip to stretch it. As time goes by, the woman puts larger and larger plates in until her lip is huge. This may not seem the most attractive fashion in the world but it means a lot to the Surma men. The larger a woman's lower lip, the higher the bride-price she can demand.

Death

The rites of passage we have looked at so far have been happy occasions, causes for celebration and festivity. But at the end of every person's life comes the sadness of death. When a friend or relation dies, the people left behind have to cope with a mixture of emotions – shock at the death, grief at the loss.

There is also an element of fear because death is an aspect of existence that we cannot fully explain. A person who is dying may feel afraid and uncertain as the time approaches. What will death be like? What happens afterwards?

People have come up with a variety of ways in which to cope with a death. The main ceremony is the funeral during which the body of the dead person is buried or cremated (burned). The funeral marks the official end of a person's life, just as the baptism or naming ceremony marks the beginning. People gather to think about the person who has died, and to remember what that person was like during life. A priest or chosen friends may speak about him or her, and the funeral may contain favourite hymns, songs, prayers or poems.

Christians, Jews and Muslims believe that a person only lives one life on Earth, but that the souls of the dead go to heaven if they have led good lives and are punished if they have not. It is traditional to bury people who follow these religions, although cremation is becoming more usual among Christians. Hindus, Sikhs and Buddhists believe that the person's soul will come back in another form, and that cremation helps the soul to escape from the body.

Protection after Death

Shih Huang-Ti, the first emperor of China, was so afraid of death that he spent most of his life preparing for it. When he became emperor in 221 BC, he ordered work on his tomb to begin. On his death in 210 BC, his body was placed in the elaborate tomb with about 6,000 life-size pottery soldiers to guard the entrance. The warrior statues, which were buried in pits, were painted in bright colours showing different uniforms and many carried weapons.

In Ancient Times

The question of what happens after death has worried people since earliest times. It is hard to accept that death is the end, and all ancient civilizations believed in some form of afterlife. People were buried with food and

FROM PREHISTORIC BURIALS *with pots and tools to the prayers that a priest says for the dying, people have always felt the need to prepare for a life after death.*

possessions to help them on the journey to the afterlife. The Neanderthals, early humans who lived between 100,000 and 40,000 years ago, seem to have been the first to bury their dead. Archaeologists have discovered burial grounds where people have been buried with tools and food which suggests that they believed in some sort of afterlife. And in some cases, the bodies were arranged in a particular way or decorated with flowers.

The ancient Egyptians believed that the afterlife was very similar to life on Earth. So people's bodies had to be preserved or 'mummified'. When a person died, the internal organs were removed and the body was packed with spices and a mineral called bitumen. Then the body was wrapped in bandages soaked in oils and resin (a natural gum), and laid in a body-shaped coffin.

Eternal Life in Peru

The Incas of Peru worshipped the Sun, and believed that their ruler, the Sapa Inca, was the Sun God. They believed that because he was a god, the Sapa Inca could not die. This belief led to a strange cult of royal ancestor worship.

When a Sapa Inca did die, his body was mummified and placed in a niche in the magnificent Coricancha temple in Cuzco, where people continued to worship him. Because he had not died, each Sapa Inca kept all his possessions and land. His successor had to start from scratch, conquering new land for the empire. Each ruler had to expand the empire, so as to acquire more land and gold.

FROM THE ANCIENT *Egyptians*
to modern Christians, the belief
in some form of afterlife has made
the last rites important to most
people. In some religions, a priest
prays with a dying person, who
then has the opportunity to confess
anything that is worrying him or
her. Medieval Christians saw the
funeral service as an entry into
the afterlife, as people still do
today. The funeral marks the
passage from the old life to the
new in many people's minds, and
although grave goods are no
longer included in many societies,
there is still the feeling of a
journey to be made. Even if people
do not believe in an afterlife, these
last rites are a vital part of
coping with bereavement.

The Afterlife

The journey to the afterlife was probably
the most important voyage a person
would ever make. Preparations for it were
elaborate. People were buried with food,
tools, weapons, jewellery and even furniture
to make sure that life in the next world was as
comfortable as possible. Entry was not
automatic, however. There could be tests
of endurance along the way and questions
might be asked at the gates. It was vitally
important to be prepared for any eventuality.

In the city of Ur, in Mesopotamia,
members of the royal family took their
servants with them to the afterlife. After the
royal body had been placed in the tomb, the
servants would follow it and swallow cups of
poison. The tomb was then sealed up.

The ancient Greeks believed that the dead
had to travel across the River Styx to the
underworld, Hades. The dead were buried
with a coin to pay Charon, the ferryman who
took them across the River Styx, and with
honey cakes for Cerberus, the three-headed
dog that guarded the gates of Hades.

The ancient Egyptians sometimes put a

plan of the route to the underworld in the coffin so that the dead did not get lost on the way. They also believed that the dead person had to go through a test before being allowed into their underworld, the kingdom of Osiris. Assessor gods would bombard the person with questions and accusations of crimes committed on Earth. The dead person would deny the crimes.

If the dead person was telling the truth, Thoth, the ibis-headed god of wisdom, would declare that he or she was 'true of voice', and the person could then enter the kingdom of Osiris. If lies were told, however,

they would be eaten by a goddess known as the 'Devourer of the Dead'.

The Vikings believed that they had to supply their own transport to the next world. Kings and queens were often buried in a longship with treasures and plenty of food. Horses and waggons were also used. Vikings who had led a good life went to Asgard where the gods lived. Warriors who died in battle went to Valhalla, a great hall in Asgard which belonged to Odin, the chief of the gods. But a Viking who died in bed went to Niflheim, a gruesome place of ice and mist, ruled over by Queen Hel.

Preparing for Death

Many religions and cultures have rituals to help a person prepare to die. Muslims are turned to face Mecca, the holy city of Islam. Roman Catholic Christians are anointed with a special oil by a priest.

In China, it was traditional to help a dying person to sit up, so that the soul could leave the body. The Murngin Aboriginals of Arnheim Land in northern Australia sing songs which tell their ancestors that another person will soon be joining them.

Grieving

When a person dies, family and friends will take some time to get over their grief. There may be a period of shock when they cannot take in the fact that the person has died. This is followed by a period of great sadness while they learn to accept life without the person.

Rituals for this period of mourning help family and friends to cope, and alert other people to what has happened. In some societies, people beat their breasts, tear their hair and wail continuously after a death. Professional mourners are sometimes brought in to add to the wailing. This ritual helps the mourners to let their emotions out. Grieving after a death is an important part of the process of recovery.

In other societies, news of a death is broken to family and close friends, and other people may be informed by a telephone call or an announcement in a newspaper. If acquaintances do not feel that they know the family well enough to visit, they may send flowers or a letter of condolence. This shows that they are thinking about the family and are ready to help if needed.

When someone dies in a Jewish household, it is traditional for the closest relatives to stay in the house. They sit on low stools while neighbours and friends come to comfort them and bring them meals. This custom is followed because close relatives are not expected to do everyday tasks when a person has died. Jews do not eat meat or drink wine for the first week after a death, and they are not supposed to go to work or listen to music. Muslim families have a similar custom. They do not cook their own meals for forty days after a death, and their food is brought in by relatives and friends. After this, the family invites friends and neighbours for a special meal which may contain the dead person's seven favourite foods.

When a Hindu dies, the family makes offerings of rice balls and milk at a shrine for the next ten days. They believe that this helps the soul to leave the body and move on to its next life.

Death is not sad for Buddhists and Sikhs because they believe that the person is one step nearer to final peace. Buddhists believe that people live several lives before they finally reach 'Nirvana', or total enlightenment.

Sikhs believe that when a person dies and is reborn, he or she is getting closer to God. When someone dies, they shout 'Waheguru' meaning 'Wonderful Lord'.

BEFORE THEIR TIME

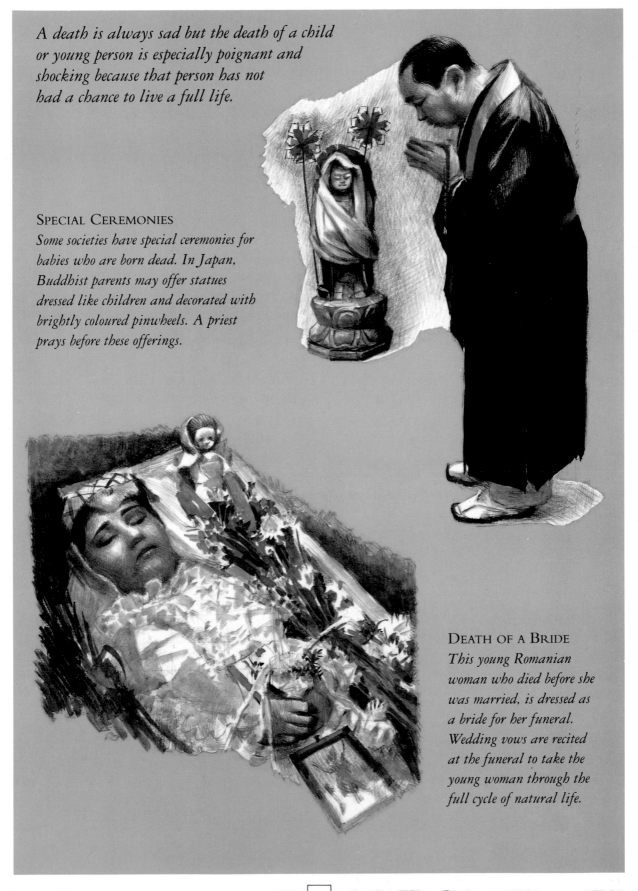

A death is always sad but the death of a child or young person is especially poignant and shocking because that person has not had a chance to live a full life.

SPECIAL CEREMONIES
Some societies have special ceremonies for babies who are born dead. In Japan, Buddhist parents may offer statues dressed like children and decorated with brightly coloured pinwheels. A priest prays before these offerings.

DEATH OF A BRIDE
This young Romanian woman who died before she was married, is dressed as a bride for her funeral. Wedding vows are recited at the funeral to take the young woman through the full cycle of natural life.

•Mourning Clothes•

Tears and shows of grief are one way of mourning. Another is wearing special clothes as a mark of respect for the dead person and also to tell other people that someone has died.

The people of the Andaman Islands in the Bay of Bengal paint their bodies with yellow and green patterns of stripes which show their relationship to the dead person. The Tiwi people of Bathurst Island off northern Australia use body paint as a disguise. They believe that the dead will try to take their friends and family with them so it is vital that they cannot tell who anyone is.

Jewish men do not shave for a week after a death and will not cut their hair for a month. Mourners in some of the Melanesian Islands shaved their heads and wore a long train of grass attached at the back of the neck and trailing down the back, almost reaching the ground. In other cultures, an all-enveloping veil was worn.

Most societies have special clothes which are a sign of mourning. Shown here are examples from around the world with the many different styles and colours that people adopt.

EUROPE ▶
The southern European widow traditionally wears a black dress, often with a black veil or headcloth. She may wear black for the rest of her life. Black has been linked with mourning in the West at least since Roman times.

INDIA ▲
Muslim women in India wear white veils for funerals.

Masters of Disguise

Today, wearing black at a funeral is a mark of respect but there used to be a more sinister reason for this garb. People believed that the ghost of the dead person was waiting to snatch someone to keep it company. If everyone wore the same drab black, it was thought, the ghost would not notice them.

It was hoped that ghosts would depart to the next world as speedily as possible. To help them, the undertaker placed pennies on the closed eyes of the dead person when he prepared the body for burial. The coins paid the spirit's fare to the next world.

◀ IRELAND
An Irish funeral procession
follows the coffin.

▼ CHINA
The Hei Miao people wear
traditional black costumes.

BATHURST ISLAND ▲
The Tiwi people disguise
themselves with body paint so the
dead cannot tell who they are.

◀ TAIWAN
A mourner wears a simple
robe made from hessian and
a white head-dress.

▲ JEWISH TRADITION
Jewish men do not shave for a
week and let their hair grow for
a month.

SULAWESI ▲
The Toradja people wear an
elaborate head-dress at funerals.

· Funerals in War Time ·

E ven in the heat of a battle, the dead need to be buried with as much dignity as possible. Sometimes the body can be flown home for a family funeral, but this is not always possible. Often people killed in action are buried on the battlefield.

When a soldier, sailor or airman is killed in a war, certain rituals are carried out, just as they are for a civilian funeral. The news is broken to the relatives, and the person's possessions are collected up and sent home. The picture shows the battlefield funeral of an American soldier killed during the Vietnam War. The war lasted for more than twenty years, from 1954 to 1975. In 1961, American soldiers were sent in to help South Vietnam in its fight against the communist north. Many young American men were drafted into the army during the Vietnam War and about 50,000 were killed.

Here, the dead soldier's comrades bow their heads in prayer as the military chaplain reads out the funeral service and prays for the dead. The grave is marked with a simple cross.

Many men and women killed in war and buried on a battlefield are later given a memorial stone in a military cemetery.

If a sailor is killed or dies on board ship, he may be buried at sea with a special funeral service carried out by the ship's captain or commander or by a priest on board.

If it is possible to organize a more formal ceremony, he or she may be given a military funeral. The coffin may be draped with the national flag, and the person's uniform hat and sometimes a weapon such as a ceremonial sword are laid on top. Comrades act as pallbearers to carry the coffin. Others may march in a procession or play ceremonial music at the funeral.

• A Jazz Funeral •
in New Orleans

People in many parts of the world adapt rituals to their own local culture. The city of New Orleans in the United States is famous for its jazz, and so it is fitting that jazz should play a part in funerals.

When a funeral procession passes through the streets of New Orleans, jazz bands of all sorts join the procession or play from the sidewalks. As the hearse travels slowly to the cemetery with the mourners following, the bands play slow, solemn music. But on the way back, the musicians break into riotous jazz that helps everyone to put their sadness behind them and look to the future with more optimism.

The idea of a happy party after a funeral is not restricted to the jazz bands of New Orleans. When a funeral is over, many people feel the need to break out of the solemnity and sadness. This is not disrespectful because it helps them to remember the person as he or she was in life.

In many countries, people hold a 'wake', a party at the family home, which may begin as a quiet and subdued gathering, but often becomes more lively as time goes by. This custom is much observed in Ireland, where sometimes the wake turns into a near riot. There are some very amusing poems and stories about the goings-on at wakes.

Some people even insist before they die that they do not want their funeral to be a sad and solemn affair because they want people to remember their life rather than their death. They ask for a ceremony of thanksgiving where they want happy songs to be sung and for friends to read favourite passages and tell amusing stories about things that happened during their life.

A Buddhist Funeral

Buddhist funerals are joyful occasions because the people believe that a person who has died is one step nearer to Nirvana. People do not usually cry and there is happy music at the funeral.

The body is usually cremated because the Buddha himself was cremated. In Burma, monks come to the funeral to comfort the mourners and to chant sacred texts to them. The family and friends make donations of food and candles to the monks. This is all supposed to help the spirit of the person who has died to be released from the body.

NORTHERN BUDDHIST FUNERAL, SIKKIM

Sikkim is a region in the Himalayan mountains in northern India. Here, the Buddhists use a funeral ritual which helps the person through the stages between death and rebirth into a new life.

THE PROCESSION
A long procession winds its way towards the funeral pyre. Someone near the front carries a parasol, which shows that the dead person is a member of the royal family. The body is carried on a bier, a covered carriage with horizontal poles which rest on the shoulders of the pallbearers. A 'lama' or priest holds a white scarf which is attached to the body.

ARRIVAL AT THE PYRE
The procession is welcomed by a blast on trumpets as it arrives at the pyre. The pyre is a stone or mud-brick structure with an open top and a hollow inside where the fire is lit. The bier is placed on the pyre and wreaths of flowers are laid around the base.

LIGHTING THE PYRE
The fire is lit and offerings of holy oil and melted, strained butter are poured on from pans on long poles. The monks, who here are wearing red robes rather than the orange robes of other regions, chant as the body falls into the flames.

A Hindu Funeral

Hindus believe that the soul of a person returns to Earth many times, although not necessarily in a human body. They also believe that the type of body they will get next time around depends on the way they have behaved in their present life. Cremation is an essential part of the funeral ceremony because a person's soul is thought to be trapped in the skull at death. It must be released by burning in the sacred fire.

The body is wrapped in a cloth and laid in a coffin which is carried to the funeral pyre by six male relatives. Before the fire is lit, a male relative, preferably the eldest son, walks round the pyre three, five or seven times holding a piece of burning wood. Then, he lights the fire as the sons of the dead person pray for the souls of their ancestors. Only a son can perform this ritual, so having male children is very important to Hindus.

Three days after the cremation, the family collect the ashes and scatter them on a river. If possible, all Hindus will have their ashes scattered on the River Ganges, which is their holy river.

Together in Death

Hindu women once followed a grim practice of hurling themselves on to the funeral pyre of their husbands. This custom, known as performing 'suttee', was supposed to wipe out the woman's sins and those of her husband. If a woman refused to go through with it, she was treated as an outcast for the rest of her life. This practice was officially abolished by the British in 1829, but it continued in some parts of India for at least another thirty years.

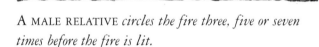

A MALE RELATIVE *circles the fire three, five or seven times before the fire is lit.*

•A Funeral on Bathurst Island•

A rt plays an important part in the lives of Australian Aboriginals and this is reflected in the rituals at a funeral of one of the Tiwi people of Bathurst Island, off northern Australia.

CEREMONIAL POSTS

A skilled carver will make ceremonial posts out of bloodwood — as many as twelve posts for one funeral. Then they are blackened in a fire, ready for painting. An artist draws special designs on each post with pigments like ochre and pipeclay mixed with water.

PROTECTIVE DISGUISES

Tiwi people believe that if they do not disguise themselves, the spirit of the deceased will try to take them away with him, so elaborate face painting is an important part of preparation. Men may stiffen their beards with sticky sap or wear false beards.

DANCING

There are many dances at the funeral. In one, a ceremonial basket is left on the grave. Some dances portray the ancestor spirits of the people taking part. As the ceremony reaches a climax, some people may cut their heads with knives, and break down in grief.

• The Mound Builders •

Native Americans live in parts of Canada, the United States and Central and South America. We know a lot about the early civilizations of Central and South America, such as the Aztecs and the Incas, but less is known about the early North American natives. They did not form great civilizations with public buildings, but lived in villages or as travelling tribes. Nor did they leave written records. However, they did leave some unique constructions – their massive burial mounds.

Between 1000 BC and AD 1450, three main Native American cultures lived in the east of North America. They were the Adena and the Hopewell peoples, both named after sites where their remains were found, and the Mississippian people.

The burial mounds of the Adena began as simple graves for a single person or family. As more people were buried on top of one another, the earthworks grew more and more massive. The bodies of important people were put into burial chambers built in the mound, with possessions such as bracelets, shells and masks.

The Hopewell people carried on the mound-building tradition but their earthworks became more and more complex. Mound City, in Ohio, is an enclosure containing twenty-four massive burial mounds. The average mound is about nine metres high and thirty metres across, and it would have taken at least 200,000 hours to move this amount of earth with simple tools. By the time of the Hopewells, funerals were quite elaborate – the bodies were put into tombs lined with wood inside special burial houses.

The Mississippian culture went even further by building temples and houses on their flat-topped mounds. Cahokia, the largest town built in prehistoric America, lies under the modern city of St Louis in Missouri. About 900 years ago, over 30,000 people lived there.

IN NORTH-WESTERN AMERICA, *his widows mourn a chief. His body has been placed on a canoe with his head pointing towards the sea. These structures are known as platform graves.*

·Keeping Watch over the Dead·

The time which passes between death and the funeral varies in different societies and religions. Jewish law states that people should be buried within twenty-four hours of death if possible. In the Christian church, a few days are allowed while families organize the funeral. In other societies, the body is not buried or cremated until it has lain in the family house for some time, so that people can see it.

SMALL NAMBA PEOPLE OF MALEKULA

The Small Namba people of the Pacific island of Malekula in the Vanuatu Republic (formerly the New Hebrides) have many rituals connected with the spirit world, particularly where funerals are concerned.

MASK OF DEATH

The body of the deceased lies on a funeral platform for a year. The skull is removed from the body and covered with a mixture of reddish clay and plant fibres, modelled to look like the person's face. A body made of wood is attached to the skull and decorated with patterns which show the social rank of the dead person.

A 'spirit' appears from the jungle dressed in leaves that have been blackened with smoke. Its head is shrouded in spider's webs. Three similar 'spirits' appear accompanied by two men painted red and white. The painted men whip the mourners until they and the 'spirits' are given yams and depart. A pig is killed and a piece of meat is given to everyone there. This is the end of the ceremony.

TORADJA PEOPLE OF SULAWESI

The body of a high-ranking Toradja man from Sulawesi in Indonesia will lie in state in his own house for several months before his funeral takes place.

OFFERINGS

Hundreds of people come to the funeral, bringing buffaloes or pigs strung up on poles. As they arrive, the guests walk in procession around the central area of the village. People in brightly coloured head-dresses perform songs and dances. These are prayers to the ancestor spirits but they are also very entertaining.

OFFICIAL DEATH

Meanwhile, the dead man is still lying in his house, as he has done for months. Four men take his body and toss it into the air, chanting as they do so. Then, they lay the body on the floor with its feet pointing south towards heaven. The man is now truly dead. He will lie here for several more months.

BURIAL

The burial takes place months later. The remains are put into a red and gold funeral bag. Along with a statue of the dead man, they are carried up a pole to a grave in the cliff side.

Many cultures believe that it is necessary to guard a body at all times until the funeral. There are various reasons for 'keeping a vigil'. Some of the peoples of Indonesia believe that a vigil helps the soul to recover from the shock of dying. In other societies, people are guarding the body from attacks by evil spirits.

A vigil also helps people to get used to the fact that the person is dead. The thought of a dead body can seem frightening, but if people can see it and get used to it lying there, it may help them to come to terms with the death. Helping to prepare the body for the funeral by washing it and clothing it in a shroud, can have the same effect.

Remembering the Dead

People want to remember people who have died long after the funeral is over. They can remember them in their own minds, of course, but many people want to make the memory more public. In the Christian Church, a memorial service is sometimes held soon after the person has died. This is a remembrance of the person's life and the things that they did in it.

Tending a grave is another way of remembering the dead person. Many people visit a family grave each week or on the anniversary of the person's death, to tidy up the ground and leave flowers on the grave. Roman Catholics may light a candle in church on the anniversary of a death.

Muslims read the Qur'an for forty days after a death in the family. The relatives take it in turns to read, and they read the book right through as many times as they can in the time. They also read the Qur'an from beginning to end each year on the anniversary of the death. In the Jewish religion, it is a duty to remember a relative who has died. On the anniversary of the death, the relatives light a candle which burns for twenty-four hours. The family also say the 'kaddish', a special prayer for the dead.

The Chinese have several special days for remembering their ancestors. The most important of these is 'Qing Ming', the Festival of Pure Brightness. On this day, people visit the tombs of their ancestors, carry out repairs, tidy up the graves and offer sacrifices. During the seventh month, families make offerings at temples and shrines to prevent harmful ghosts and spirits from attacking the spirits of their ancestors. In the tenth month, families leave paper clothes and money on the tombs in case the ancestors need them in the afterlife.

A Loaf of Bread

Orthodox Christians invite people to a memorial service for the dead person by giving them a loaf of bread. The mourners are also given a special type of porridge made from wheat at the service. The wheat is a symbol of the food people eat during their lives. Once people have died, they no longer need the food, so giving it away helps the soul to go on to its new life.

The Day of the Dead

One of the strangest memorial traditions is the Day of the Dead, *El Dia de los Muertas*, which is celebrated in Mexico on 2 November, the day known as All Souls' Day in other Christian countries. All Souls' Day is the time when Christians traditionally pray for the dead, whose souls are supposed to be about on that day.

No one would call it a jolly occasion, except the Mexicans. They believe that the spirits of the dead return to Earth on the Day of the Dead, but they are not frightened by the fact. To them, it is a cause for celebration, and the dead are given a joyous welcome. Children receive presents of grinning skulls made of sugar, and chocolate coffins with their own names on them. Families keep an all-night vigil at the graveside, but they do not find it spooky. They talk to the dead and sing songs as they munch the picnics they have brought with them.

Mexico is a Roman Catholic country, but the people's casual attitude towards death goes back to long before the Spaniards arrived to convert the people to Christianity, and even before the time of the Aztecs or Mayans.

Archaeologists have discovered that the Totonaca, a tribe of Native Americans who lived in Mexico between the third and eighth centuries AD, believed that the dead went to an underworld which was very similar to the living world. The dead would repeat their earthly lives so exactly that there was no reason to fear death.

ON EL DIA *de los Muertas, the Day of the Dead, Mexicans gather in cemeteries for a celebration. Masks and dolls on the theme of death are for sale.*

• Marking the Grave •

The most lasting memorial to a person's life is the marking of his or her grave. Whether the grave is marked with a simple stone or an elaborately carved monument, it tells you who is buried there and it lasts for centuries.

People who are cremated have no grave, of course, but a plaque set into a memorial wall at a Garden of Remembrance serves the same purpose as a gravestone. It is a place where people can come to pay their respects, lay flowers and think of the person in life.

People have many different ways of marking graves throughout the world. Some memorials are made of stone, others are made of wood. Some are plain and simple, others are carved or painted in bright colours. Sometimes, people are buried in huge, ornate family tombs and vaults. Others may have a memorial plaque inside a church. But whatever form the memorial takes, it is an important tribute to the person's life.

FRANCE ▶

These tall cemetery lantern towers are seen in some parts of France. The cone-shaped cap originally contained a light which was always kept alight to mark the holy ground where the dead were buried.

▼ TURKEY

Muslims are buried with their right side turned towards Mecca and their gravestones also face Mecca. The stones are decorated with inscriptions and carved patterns of leaves and fruit.

▲ TIBET
High in the Himalayan mountains, Buddhist graves are marked with piles of stones and flags inscribed with prayers.

◄ BORNEO

The Dusun people of coastal Borneo mark their graves with brightly decorated wooden canopies.

▼ CHINA

Tall towers marked graveyards in China during the early twentieth century. Modern tombs may be smaller and lower.

▲ EUROPE

Crosses are the traditional markers for Christian graves. The stone will be marked with the person's name and their dates of birth and death, together with a short tribute or 'epitaph' from the family.

▲ CENTRAL ASIA

Muslim nomads who live in the Pamir mountains of Eastern Turkestan build mosque-like tombs for their dead.

Find Out Some More

BOOKS TO READ

Birth Customs by Lucy Rushton (Wayland, 1992)

Birth Customs by Jon Mayled (Wayland 1986)

Festivals and Celebrations by Rowland Purton (Blackwell, 1983)

Festive Occasions by Judy Ridgway (Oxford University Press, 1988)

Growing up in Islam by J. Ardavan (Longman, 1990)

Jewish Festivals by Jane Cooper (Wayland, 1989)

Marriage Customs by Anita Compton (Wayland, 1992)

Marriage Customs by Jon Mayled (Wayland, 1986)

Mazal-Tov, A Jewish Wedding by Jose Patterson (Hamish Hamilton, 1988)

Muslim Festivals by Jane Cooper (Wayland, 1989)

Religions of the World by Lynn Underwood (Belitha Press, 1991)

Religious Services by Jon Mayled (Wayland, 1986)

Sikh Festivals by Dr Sukhbir Singh Kapoor (Wayland, 1985)

The Sikh World by Daljit Singh and Angela Smith (Simon and Schuster Young Books, 1992)

PLACES TO VISIT

Some museums have displays which show how people dealt with rites of passage in the past. For example, the British Museum has examples of mummification in Ancient Egypt. Other museums have grave goods on display.

- The British Museum, Great Russell Street, London WC1B 3DG. Telephone: 0171–636 1555.
- The Museum of Mankind displays artefacts from traditional cultures around the world. Its address is 6 Burlington Gardens, London W1X 2EX. Telephone: 0171–437 2224.
- University Museum of Archaeology and Anthropology, Downing Street, Cambridge CB1 Telephone: 01223–337733
- The Pitt-Rivers Museum, Parks Rd, Oxford OX1 3PP. Telephone: 01865–270949.
- Royal Museum of Scotland, Chambers Street, Edinburgh EH1 1JF. Telephone: 0131–225 7534.

RELIGIOUS CEREMONIES

Most religions welcome interested inquirers. But please remember that some religious ceremonies, like marriages and funerals, have intense personal meaning to those involved. Don't push in where you are unwelcome.

- Nowadays baptisms are often performed during a Sunday morning service, so you can ring the local church and ask when next baptisms are to be performed.
- Ask your teacher if he or she could arrange a visit to the local synagogue or mosque. It is best to make an official visit as you don't want to upset people by not behaving suitably in their holy place.
- The Sikh Missionary Society, 10 Featherstone Road, Southall, Middlesex UB2 5AA can be contacted about visits to a gurdwara.

If you are going abroad on holiday, look out for unusual marriage customs, ways of conducting a funeral, and listen to what the guide may tell you about places you may visit. However, please remember that it is their country and ritual and don't take photographs or push in to take a closer look if they ask you not to.

Index